THE KEY
STUDENT STUDY GUIDE

Social Studies 6

THE KEY student study guide is designed to help students achieve success in school. The content in each study guide is 100% curriculum aligned and serves as an excellent source of material for review and practice. To create this book, teachers, curriculum specialists, and assessment experts have worked closely to develop the instructional pieces that explain each of the key concepts for the course. The practice questions and sample tests have detailed solutions that show problem-solving methods, highlight concepts that are likely to be tested, and point out potential sources of errors. **THE KEY** is a complete guide to be used by students throughout the school year for reviewing and understanding course content, and to prepare for assessments.

Publisher
Gautam Rao

Contributors
Brigitta Braden
Sharlene Jackson
James Kropfreiter

Rao, Gautam, 1961 –
THE KEY – Social Studies 6
ISBN: 978-1-77044-434-8

    1. Social Studies – Juvenile Literature. I. Title

Published by
Castle Rock Research Corp.
2000 First & Jasper
10065 Jasper Avenue
Edmonton, AB T5J 3B1

   10 9

Dedicated to the memory of Dr. V. S. Rao

THE KEY—Social Studies 6

THE KEY consists of the following sections:

KEY Tips for Being Successful at School gives examples of study and review strategies. It includes information about learning styles, study schedules, and note taking for test preparation.

Class Focus includes a unit on each area of the curriculum. Units are divided into sections, each focusing on one of the specific expectations, or main ideas, that students must learn about in that unit. Examples, definitions, and visuals help to explain each main idea. Practice questions on the main ideas are also included. At the end of each unit is a test on the important ideas covered. The practice questions and unit tests help students identify areas they know and those they need to study more. They can also be used as preparation for tests and quizzes. Most questions are of average difficulty, though some are easy and some are hard. Each unit is prefaced by a ***Table of Correlations,*** which correlates questions in the unit to the specific curriculum expectations. Answers and solutions are found at the end of each unit.

KEY Strategies for Success on Tests helps students get ready for tests. It shows students different types of questions they might see, word clues to look for when reading them, and hints for answering them.

Practice Tests includes one to three tests based on the entire course. They are very similar to the format and level of difficulty that students may encounter on final tests. In some regions, these tests may be reprinted versions of official tests, or reflect the same difficulty levels and formats as official versions. This gives students the chance to practice using real world examples. Answers and complete solutions are provided at the end of the section.

For the complete curriculum document (including specific expectations along with examples and sample problems), visit http://education.alberta.ca/teachers/program/socialstudies/programs.aspx.

THE KEY *Study Guides* are available for many courses. Check www.castlerockresearch.com for a complete listing of books available for your area.

For information about any of our resources or services, please call Castle Rock Research at 780.448.9619 or visit our website at http://www.castlerockresearch.com.

At Castle Rock Research, we strive to produce an error-free resource. If you should find an error, please contact us so that future editions can be corrected.

TABLE OF CONTENTS

NOTES

iv

KEY Tips for Being Successful at School

⚷ *KEY* TIPS FOR BEING SUCCESSFUL AT SCHOOL

KEY FACTORS CONTRIBUTING TO SCHOOL SUCCESS

In addition to learning the content of your courses, there are some other things that you can do to help you do your best at school. Some of these strategies are listed below.

- **Keep a positive attitude:** Always reflect on what you can already do and what you already know.

- **Be prepared to learn**: Have ready the necessary pencils, pens, notebooks, and other required materials for participating in class.

- **Complete all of your assignments:** Do your best to finish all of your assignments. Even if you know the material well, practice will reinforce your knowledge. If an assignment or question is difficult |for you, work through it as far as you can so that your teacher can see exactly where you are having difficulty.

- **Set small goals for yourself when you are learning new material:** For example, when learning the parts of speech, do not try to learn everything in one night. Work on only one part or section each study session. When you have memorized one particular part of speech and understand it, then move on to another one, continue this process until you have memorized and learned all the parts of speech.

- **Review your classroom work regularly at home:** Review to be sure that you understand the material that you learned in class.

- **Ask your teacher for help**: Your teacher will help you if you do not understand something or if you are having a difficult time completing your assignments.

- **Get plenty of rest and exercise:** Concentrating in class is hard work. It is important to be well-rested and have time to relax and socialize with your friends. This helps you to keep your positive attitude about your school work.

- **Eat healthy meals:** A balanced diet keeps you healthy and gives you the energy that you need for studying at school and at home.

 **HOW TO FIND YOUR LEARNING STYLE**

Every student learns differently. The manner in which you learn best is called your learning style. By knowing your learning style, you can increase your success at school. Most students use a combination of learning styles. Do you know what type of learner you are? Read the following descriptions. Which of these common learning styles do you use most often?

- Do you need to say things out loud? You may learn best by saying, hearing, and seeing words. You are probably really good at memorizing things such as dates, places, names, and facts. You may need to write and then say out loud the steps in a process, a formula, or the actions that lead up to a significant event.

- Do you need to read or see things? You may learn best by looking at and working with pictures. You are probably really good at puzzles, imagining things, and reading maps and charts. You may need to use strategies like mind mapping and webbing to organize your information and study notes.

- Do you need to draw or write things down? You may learn best by touching, moving, and figuring things out using manipulatives. You are probably really good at physical activities and learning through movement. You may need to draw your finger over a diagram to remember it, "tap out" the steps needed to solve a problem, or "feel" yourself writing or typing a formula.

SCHEDULING STUDY TIME

You should review your class notes regularly to ensure that you have a clear understanding of all the new material you learned. Reviewing your lessons on a regular basis helps you to learn and remember ideas and concepts. It also reduces the quantity of material that you need to study prior to a test. Establishing a study schedule will help you to make the best use of your time.

Regardless of the type of study schedule you use, you may want to consider the following suggestions to maximize your study time and effort:

- Organize your work so that you begin with the most challenging material first.

- Divide the subject's content into small, manageable chunks.

- Alternate regularly between your different subjects and types of study activities in order to maintain your interest and motivation.

- Make a daily list with headings like "Must Do," "Should Do," and "Could Do."

- Begin each study session by quickly reviewing what you studied the day before.

- Maintain your usual routine of eating, sleeping, and exercising to help you concentrate better for extended periods of time.

CREATING STUDY NOTES

MIND-MAPPING OR WEBBING

- Use the key words, ideas, or concepts from your reading or class notes to create a mind map or web (a diagram or visual representation of the given information). A mind map or web is sometimes referred to as a knowledge map.

- Write the key word, concept, theory, or formula in the centre of your page.

- Write down related facts, ideas, events, and information and then link them to the central concept with lines.

- Use coloured markers, underlining, or other symbols to emphasize things such as relationships, time lines, and important information.

- The following mind map is an example of one that could help you develop an essay:

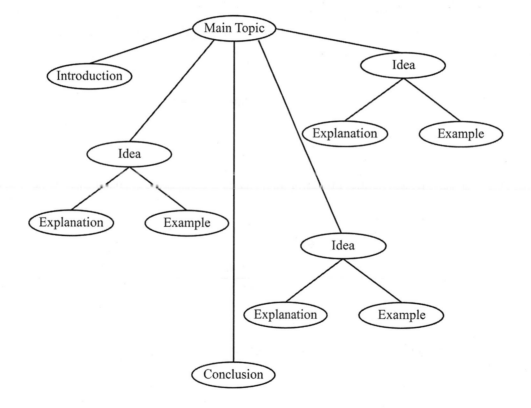

INDEX CARDS

To use index cards while studying, follow these steps:

- Write a key word or question on one side of an index card.

- On the reverse side, write the definition of the word, answer to the question, or any other important information that you want to remember.

What are the levels of
government in Canada?

What are the levels of government in Canada?

The levels of government in
Canada are federal, provincial/territorial,
and municipal.

SYMBOLS AND STICKY NOTES—IDENTIFYING IMPORTANT INFORMATION

- Use symbols to mark your class notes. For example, an exclamation mark (!) might be used to point out something that must be learned well because it is a very important idea. A question mark (?) may highlight something that you are not certain about, and a diamond (◊) or asterisk (*) could highlight interesting information that you want to remember.

- Use sticky notes when you are not allowed to put marks in books.

- Use sticky notes to mark a page in a book that contains an important diagram, formula, explanation, etc.

- Use sticky notes to mark important facts in research books.

MEMORIZATION TECHNIQUES

- Association relates new learning to something you already know. For example, to remember the spelling difference between dessert and desert, recall that the word sand has only one s. So, because there is sand in a desert, the word desert only has on s.

- Mnemonic devices are sentences that you create to remember a list or group of items. For example, the first letter of each word in the phrase "**E**very **G**ood **B**oy **D**eserves **F**udge" helps you to remember the names of the lines on the treble clef staff (E, G, B, D, and F) in music.

- Acronyms are words that are formed from the first letters or parts of the words in a group. For example, **RADAR** is actually an acronym for **Ra**dio **D**etecting **A**nd **R**anging, and **MASH** is an acronym for **M**obile **A**rmy **S**urgical **H**ospital. **HOMES** helps you to remember the names of the five Great Lakes (**H**uron, **O**ntario, **M**ichigan, **E**rie, and **S**uperior).

- Visualizing requires you to use your mind's eye to "see" a chart, list, map, diagram, or sentence as it is in your textbook or notes, on the chalk board or computer screen, or in a display.

- Initialisms are abbreviations that are formed from the first letters or parts of the words in a group. Unlike acronyms, initialisms cannot be pronounced as a word themselves. For example, **BEDMAS** is an initialism for the order of operations in math (**B**rackets, **E**xponents, **D**ivide, **M**ultiply, **A**dd, **S**ubtract).

KEY STRATEGIES FOR REVIEWING

Reviewing textbook material, class notes, and handouts should be an ongoing activity. Spending time reviewing becomes more critical when you are preparing for tests. You may find some of the following review strategies useful when studying during your scheduled study time.

- Before reading a selection, preview it by noting the headings, charts, graphs, and chapter questions.

- Read the complete introduction to identify the key information that is addressed in the selection.

- Read the first sentence of the next paragraph for the main idea.

- Skim the paragraph and note the key words, phrases, and information.

- Read the last sentence of the paragraph.

- Repeat this process for each paragraph and section until you have skimmed the entire selection.

KEY STRATEGIES FOR SUCCESS: A CHECKLIST

Review, review, review: review is a huge part of doing well at school and preparing for tests. Here is a checklist for you to keep track of how many suggested strategies for success you are using. Read each question and then put a check mark (✓) in the correct column. Look at the questions where you have checked the "No" column. Think about how you might try using some of these strategies to help you do your best at school.

KEY Strategies for Success	Yes	No
Do you attend school regularly?		
Do you know your personal learning style—how you learn best?		
Do you spend 15 to 30 minutes a day reviewing your notes?		
Do you study in a quiet place at home?		
Do you clearly mark the most important ideas in your study notes?		
Do you use sticky notes to mark texts and research books?		
Do you practise answering multiple-choice and written-response questions?		
Do you ask your teacher for help when you need it?		
Are you maintaining a healthy diet and sleep routine?		
Are you participating in regular physical activity?		

Citizens Participating in Decision-Making

CITIZENS PARTICIPATING IN DECISION-MAKING

Table of Correlations			
Specific Expectation	**Practice Questions**	**Unit Test Questions**	**Practice Test**
Students will:			
6.1.2 *Demonstrate an understanding of the fundamental principles of democracy by exploring and reflecting upon the following questions and issues:*			
6.1.2.1 *What is democracy?*	1, 2	1	2
6.1.2.2 *What are the similarities and differences between direct and representative democracy?*	3	2, 3	1, 3
6.1.2.3 *What are the rights and responsibilities of citizens living in a representative democracy?*	4	4	WR1
6.1.2.4 *How does Canada's justice system help protect your democratic and constitutional rights?*	5	5	4, 5
6.1.3 *Analyze how the democratic ideals of equity and fairness have influenced legislation in Canada over time by exploring and reflecting upon the following questions and issues:*			
6.1.3.1 *How does the Canadian Charter of Rights and Freedoms protect the individual rights and freedoms of all Canadians?*	6, 7	6	6, 48
6.1.3.2 *How does the Canadian Charter of Rights and Freedoms protect collective rights in Canada?*	8, 9		9, 49, 50
6.1.3.3 *How did the Treaty of La Grande Paix de Montréal address collective identity and collective rights?*	10	7	7, 8
6.1.3.4 *How do the Treaty of La Grande Paix de Montréal and the Canadian Charter of Rights and Freedoms compare in the way each addresses individual and collective identity and collective rights?*	11	8	
6.1.3.5 *Why is the Canadian Charter of Rights and Freedoms entrenched in the Canadian Constitution?*	12	9	
6.1.4 *Analyze the structure and functions of local governments in Alberta by exploring and reflecting upon the following questions and issues:*			
6.1.4.1 *How are representatives chosen to form a local government?*	13, 14	10	
6.1.4.2 *What are the responsibilities of local governments?*	15, 16	11, 12	10, 11
6.1.4.3 *How are local governments structured differently in rural and urban settings?*	17	13, 14	
6.1.4.4 *What role is played by school boards within local communities?*	18	15	12, 13

6.1.5	Analyze the structure and functions of Alberta's provincial government by exploring and reflecting upon the following questions and issues:			
6.1.5.1	How is the provincial government structured?	19	16, 17	14, 17
6.1.5.2	What is the role and status of the lieutenant-governor within the provincial government?	20	18	15, 16
6.1.5.3	What are the responsibilities of the provincial government?	21, 22, 23	19, 20	18
6.1.5.4	How are representatives chosen at the provincial level of government?	24		
6.1.5.5	What are the differences between the responsibilities of a Member of the Legislative Assembly (MLA) and a cabinet minister?	25	21	
6.1.6	Analyze how individuals, groups and associations within a community impact decision making of local and provincial governments by exploring and reflecting upon the following questions and issues:			
6.1.6.1	How can individuals, groups, and associations within a community participate in the decision-making process regarding current events or issues (i.e., lobbying, petitioning, organizing and attending local meetings and rallies, contacting elected representatives)?	26, 27	22, 23	20, 21, 27, WR2
6.1.6.2	How do associations such as the Association canadienne-francaise de l'Alberta (ACFA), the Metis Nation of Alberta Association (MNAA), and the First Nations Authorities (FNA) provide their members with a voice at local and provincial levels to exercise historical and constitutional rights?	28, 29	24	19, 22, 23, 24, 25, 26
6.1.6.3	In what ways do elected officials demonstrate their accountability to the electorate?	30	25	

CITIZENS PARTICIPATING IN DECISION-MAKING

6.1.2.1 What is democracy?

WHAT IS DEMOCRACY?

Democracy is a form of government in which the power resides in the people. The words *justice, equity, freedom,* and *representation* are all a part of democracy. Democracy is a political system that holds elections and protects the rights and freedoms of the people. In a democracy, the citizens are represented and have a voice in decision-making. People living in a particular society have certain beliefs about how they should behave. Democratic principles are really a reflection of the values or beliefs held by the citizens who live in that democracy. Some of these shared values include fairness, respect for differences, equality, the right to vote, peacefulness, compromise, and the inclusion of differing points of view. The values of the people help the government make decisions that affect the people and the country as a whole.

In Canada, democracy and the democratic rights of Canadians are based on and supported by these four principles:

- Equity and equal opportunity for all

- Freedom of speech, thought, and religion

- Justice and fairness for all groups and individuals

- Representation by elected individuals voted into office by Canadians to act on their behalf

In a democratic country such as Canada, decision-making is done by the voters. Even though decisions are made by the majority, the rights of the minority are also respected. Occasionally, when a decision is made by the majority, a significant number of people do not support it. In our country, minorities can join with others who agree with them and try to change or influence the way the majority views a particular issue.

Canada is a democratic country with three levels of government that address the many needs of the people. These levels of government are local (municipal), provincial, and federal. Each level of government has elected or appointed citizens who represent the opinions of the people in their community, province or territory, and country. These elected representatives carry out the business of government.

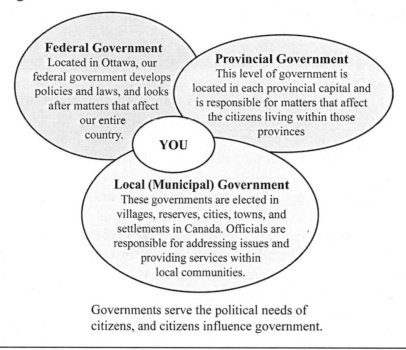

Federal Government
Located in Ottawa, our federal government develops policies and laws, and looks after matters that affect our entire country.

Provincial Government
This level of government is located in each provincial capital and is responsible for matters that affect the citizens living within those provinces

YOU

Local (Municipal) Government
These governments are elected in villages, reserves, cities, towns, and settlements in Canada. Officials are responsible for addressing issues and providing services within local communities.

Governments serve the political needs of citizens, and citizens influence government.

Practice Questions: 1, 2

6.1.2.2 What are the similarities and differences between direct and representative democracy?

DIRECT AND REPRESENTATIVE DEMOCRACY

Democracy in Canada allows all citizens to participate in government matters that influence their communities and country. Decisions are made with the intent of benefiting the common good and making communities better places to live.

All citizens have the opportunity to take part in government matters. However, it is not reasonable or practical to expect all citizens to do so. Travelling great distances to meetings may be inconvenient for some. Many citizens may not have the time required for such participation because of their jobs and other obligations. Also, it would be difficult to make decisions when so many voices would need to be heard. Imagine if all the citizens of Alberta travelled to the Legislature in Edmonton to take part in all the decision-making. There would be thousands of voices to be heard. Decisions would take forever! Instead, **representative democracy** allows citizens to use their right to vote to elect a representative who will express their concerns and make political decisions for them. The candidate who receives the most votes from the citizens living in a given area becomes their representative in government. This happens in all three types of elections: municipal, provincial, and federal. When your parents and guardians vote in elections, they are taking part in the process of representative democracy. Perhaps you would like to find out who the government representative is for your family and neighbourhood at the municipal, provincial, and federal levels.

As Grade 6 students, you are not old enough to vote for representatives in government. However, you and your friends may have participated in representative democracy under other circumstances. Many schools have student representatives in each grade or classroom. These students represent their classes in school matters that involve student decision-making, such as planning school events or charity fundraising. Often, there is an election in each classroom. Each class nominates candidates, conducts a vote, and determines the class representative. The chosen person then represents the wishes and viewpoints of the class.

In a **direct democracy**, government is based on the citizens themselves voting directly on political matters. Canadian democracy has its origins in the direct democracy practiced in ancient Athens. There, it was considered the responsibility of male citizens to actively take part in Athenian government within the Assembly. To participate, they had to be of at least 20 years of age and have completed military service. There were thousands of male citizens who attended open-area assembly meetings in Athens atop the Pnyx. All had the equal right to speak and vote on matters by a show of hands. On occasion, voting was done by placing a coloured stone that represented their decision into a jug. Male citizens of 30 years or older were also expected to serve mandatory terms on the Council of 500 or take part in jury duty within Athenian courts. Ancient Athenian government believed that direct democracy provided equal justice and peace to all by basing political power in the hands of many people instead of a few. Today in Canada, our form of political democracy differs from that of ancient Athens in several ways. In ancient Athens, not all citizens could vote, nor were they considered equal.

Though representative democracy is more practical to use for decision-making, there are instances in Canada where direct democracy is very useful and does occur. This usually happens for matters of regional or local decision-making. Referendums or plebiscites are a form of direct democracy that occur when citizens vote directly on an issue or law that concerns them. The decision to divide the Northwest Territories in two was determined by a plebiscite held in 1982. The majority of voters in that plebiscite voted in favour of dividing the Northwest Territories. This led to the creation of Nunavut in 1993. Later, Iqaluit was chosen as capital of the new territory of Nunavut by another plebiscite in 1995.

If you have ever been on a sports team, it is possible that the coaches have asked you and your teammates to choose a team name. You and your teammates probably made some suggestions and then voted. The name you chose was based on the wishes of the majority of players on the team. In a case like this, you and your teammates would have taken part in a form of direct democracy.

Practice Question: 3

6.1.2.3 What are the rights and responsibilities of citizens living in a representative democracy?

THE RIGHTS AND RESPONSIBILITIES OF CITIZENS IN A REPRESENTATIVE DEMOCRACY

Every citizen in Canada has certain rights and responsibilities that are considered fair and just for everyone. All Canadians have essential rights that are protected by the Canadian Charter of Rights and Freedoms. This is a document of 34 sections that is firmly entrenched within the Constitution of Canada. These essential rights include the freedom of speech, thought, and religion and the right to vote. In Canada, many laws have been designed to protect people's rights and freedoms and the environment.

There is a relationship that occurs between rights and responsibilities. A right has a responsibility attached to it. For example, in Canada, every citizen has the right to be viewed as equal under the law. Every person also has a responsibility to obey the laws of our country. If a law is viewed as unfair by an individual or group, the person or group can express that opinion to the appropriate level of government. While all Canadians have the right to freedom of expression, they also have a responsibility. Your freedom of expression must not be offensive or disrespectful to the rights and freedoms of other citizens expressing their viewpoints. Canadian citizens have rights in the Charter, but also have the responsibility to treat others with respect and seek to eliminate discrimination and injustice.

As Canada is a representative democracy, everyone living in the country has the opportunity and right to vote for representatives at each level of government. The only condition is that the voter must be an adult and a Canadian citizen. However, Canadian citizens must try to understand the issues that representatives are supporting to be well-informed electors at election time. Thus, Canadians have both the right to vote and the responsibility to vote wisely.

In a representative democracy such as Canada's, citizens have a responsibility to express their political needs and concerns to their government representatives. This input is necessary so government representatives have the information necessary to make effective decisions. Since all citizens are affected by the decisions, all citizens must help the government learn what is needed.

In a democracy like Canada's, all citizens receive particular democratic rights, but citizens also have a responsibility to participate in and contribute to the betterment of society. Citizens who volunteer to improve the quality of life of others, their communities, and their environment contribute greatly to making our country a better place for all. These volunteer actions contribute to the common good of all citizens. Canadians, including yourself and your peers, can make valuable contributions by volunteering in your community and taking part in activities that help others. You can also help by addressing situations that concern you or that you believe are unfair and need change.

Practice Question: 4

6.1.2.4 How does Canada's justice system help protect your democratic and constitutional rights?

CANADA'S JUSTICE SYSTEM

Just as rules are necessary for games and sports matches, a democratic society needs laws to function properly. These laws are needed to resolve conflicts, protect democratic and constitutional rights, and help groups of people live together peacefully. Therefore, laws are passed by Canada's justice system to govern the behaviour of people, to protect people's democratic and constitutional rights, and to protect the environment.

The democratic and constitutional rights of all Canadian citizens are protected by the Canadian Charter of Rights and Freedoms, which is entrenched in Canada's Constitution. The Canadian Constitution is our country's supreme document. It defines our nation and contains our country's main laws. These laws, which reflect Canadian values such as fairness, respect, equality, and peacefulness, are necessary to maintain order in our society and protect the rights of Canadian citizens. Canada's justice system seeks to protect these rights by ensuring that laws are respected and obeyed and the rights and freedoms of the Charter are upheld. Some rights in Canada are not addressed in the Charter but do exist elsewhere in provincial legislation. Within the Canadian government, it is the job of the justice system to protect the freedoms and rights of all Canadians.

Sometimes, existing laws need to be examined to see that they respect and are not in conflict with the rights and freedoms guaranteed in the Canadian Charter of Rights and Freedoms. For example, the Supreme Court of Canada can be appealed to in order to examine and interpret whether a provincial law or a provincial court ruling (decision) toward an individual or group of citizens upholds their individual rights and freedoms stipulated in the Charter. If the Supreme Court decides that the law in question ignores the rights stated in the Charter, then that provincial law becomes invalid. When the Charter is challenged, Canadian courts make the final decisions, not the government. Consequently, laws are sometimes changed or struck down in order to protect the democratic and constitutional rights of all citizens. Maintaining the rights and freedoms of Canadian citizens and protecting the common good is the backbone of our Canadian democratic system.

Practice Question: 5

6.1.3.1 How does the Canadian Charter of Rights and Freedoms protect the individual rights and freedoms of all Canadians?

THE CANADIAN CHARTER OF RIGHTS AND FREEDOMS

The majority of the rights and freedoms discussed in the Canadian Charter of Rights and Freedoms refer to the individual rights and freedoms of all Canadians. These individual rights and freedoms are based on our country's democratic values of fairness, respect for differences, equality, and the right to vote. One intent of the Charter is to state and describe several groups of individual rights and freedoms that the Canadian government must protect and guarantee in order to ensure a democratic and free society. The Charter protects and guarantees the individual rights and freedoms of Canadians because the Charter is entrenched in the Constitution of Canada. Thus, the individual rights and freedoms of all Canadians are guaranteed by law.

Laws at different levels of government in Canada can be challenged if individuals or groups of citizens feel that their individual rights and freedoms have not been upheld. One issue that has been challenged in recent years concerns the right to wear cultural or religious dress while taking part in sporting events. Some provincial laws are being explored to see if they do or do not support the individual rights and freedoms that the Charter protects.

You can think of the Charter as a human rights document created by our democratic government to protect the rights and freedoms of citizens in our country. Our government, in turn, is responsible for ensuring that these rights and freedoms are protected and guaranteed.

Take a few minutes to read through a copy of the Canadian Charter of Rights and Freedoms. You will notice that the sections of the Charter serve to promote and protect the individual rights and freedoms of all Canadians. The following sections are found in the Canadian Charter of Rights and Freedoms.

Fundamental freedoms—The fundamental freedoms include the freedom of speech, thought, opinion, and religion. These freedoms, though, must be expressed in a peaceful manner. The Charter does set a degree of reasonable limitation upon individual rights to protect the rights and freedoms of all citizens. For example, a citizen's right to free speech cannot be used to make false claims that are damaging to other individuals or groups. Individual rights and freedoms can, therefore, be limited by the government if the government has a reason to do so.

Democratic rights—These rights ensure Canadians the right to vote for representatives in federal and provincial governments. Elected representatives consider the viewpoints of their constituents before making decisions. If necessary, they can refer to the Charter to be sure they are considering all groups of people fairly. Over the last century, the government has expanded the right to vote to greater numbers of citizens. During Canada's early elections, only land-owning men of European descent could vote in Canada. Some women were given the right to vote in 1918, though not in all provinces at the provincial level. Long years of protest by Canadians of a number of different ethnic backgrounds resulted in the vote being granted to greater numbers of citizens. Receiving the right to vote increased the feeling of equality among Canadians.

Democratic rights apply only to Canadian citizens.

Mobility rights—These rights allow all citizens with permanent residency status in Canada the right to live, work, and travel anywhere in the country. Mobility rights apply only to Canadian citizens.

Legal rights—These rights ensure the safety of Canadians and protect citizens involved in legal conflict. When a person is arrested, put on trial for breaking the law, or imprisoned, these rights are applied. For example, the right to be considered innocent until proven guilty in a court of law is a legal right in Canada.

Equality rights—These rights ensure equal and fair treatment to everyone. Equality rights involve treating all individuals equally regardless of religious choice, race, ethnic or national origin, cognitive or physical impairments, age, or gender. In order to ensure equity and treat people with special needs fairly, sometimes special allowances, known as accommodations, need to be made. For example, in order to give a person confined to a wheelchair the individual right to attend a school that has outside steps only, a ramp would need to be built. This accommodation simply creates a fair and equal opportunity for all persons to attend that particular school. No one attending the school is advantaged over others as a result of the ramp being built. However, without the ramp, those with particular special needs would be disadvantaged.

Official language rights—These rights are referred to in the Charter. Because Canada is a bilingual country, both French and English are officially used in all of the parliamentary and governmental institutions. Minority language education rights are also referred to in the Charter. Official education rights in school districts throughout Canada are based on references to and the guarantee of language rights that appear in the Charter.

Other Rights—Other rights refer to the various rights outlined below.

Other rights include the rights that are guaranteed to and apply to Canada's Aboriginal peoples. Previous rights and treaties granted to Aboriginal groups throughout Canadian history are also maintained in the Charter.

Other rights also include the enhancement and preservation of the multicultural heritage of Canadians. The diversity of Canadians' multicultural heritages forms part of our rich and unique Canadian identity.

Additionally, gender equality rights are also stated in the Charter. During the early 1980s, section 28 of the Charter was created. It ensured that the rights and freedoms of women and men were guaranteed to be equal regardless of gender. This ruling paved the way for women to receive equal pay for equal work. Previously, men were sometimes paid more for their work. Also, advertising work in sections of the newspaper specifically for men or for women ceased to exist. The practice became viewed as unfair and in contradiction to the newly created section 28 of the Charter.

Practice Questions: 6, 7

6.1.3.2 How does the Canadian Charter of Rights and Freedoms protect collective rights in Canada?

COLLECTIVE RIGHTS IN CANADA

Collective rights are those rights that belong to individuals who together form a particular group. These groups have a **collective identity**. They share common beliefs and often the same language, culture, and values. Additionally, these groups have a long history of seeking particular rights in Canada that goes back to before the Confederation of Canada in 1867. In seeking to ensure equality and fairness, the Charter protects the collective rights of aboriginal groups and the linguistic rights of official language minorities (English-speaking and French-speaking people) throughout Canada. When the Charter was entrenched in our Constitution in 1982, the collective rights of Aboriginal Peoples, English and French as official languages, and the language rights of minority English-speaking and French-speaking communities in Canada were also entrenched.

PROTECTING COLLECTIVE RIGHTS FOR ABORIGINAL PEOPLES

Prior to European settlement during the 17th century, Canada was inhabited by many aboriginal communities. Presently, more than one million aboriginal people, who are descendants of Canada's original inhabitants, live in our country. They comprise about 5% of our nation's total population. Aboriginal Peoples includes all Inuit, Métis, and First Nations.

Throughout Canada's history, aboriginal groups in Canada have argued that they have a rightful claim to lands they originally occupied. Many land claims have been pursued by aboriginal groups over the years prior to and since the Charter was established in 1982. In these claims, they seek to establish legal title to the areas of Canada they live in and receive financial compensation for lands they have given up. This process allows Aboriginal Peoples the opportunity to regain some of their lands, their rights, self governance, and natural resources. If aboriginal rights are to be affected by any change in the Constitution, First Nations, Inuit, and Métis groups have the right to be directly involved.

When the Charter was entrenched in the Constitution in 1982, the collective rights for aboriginal groups were guaranteed. At that point, any previous law and ruling that did not demonstrate equity for aboriginal rights could be appealed to the Supreme Court of Canada. Prior to the Charter, the Supreme Court of Canada had already ruled in 1973 that rights to traditional territories belong to Aboriginal Peoples, even where treaties did not exist.

Over 200 specific land claims concerning original treaties that have been broken or not fulfilled have been settled in Canada. Comprehensive land claims look after aboriginal claims to land, self-governance, and natural resources in areas where treaties have never existed. In 1993, after much negotiation between the Inuit and the federal government, the Nunavut Land Claim Agreement was passed. This agreement divided the Northwest Territories and created the new territory of Nunavut. Collective rights ensured that the Inuit played a strong role in shaping their territorial government.

There have been a number of important aboriginal rulings in Canada that have occurred as a result of the protection of aboriginal collective rights as stated in the Charter. For example, in British Columbia in 1997, the Supreme Court of Canada decided that (1) Aboriginal Peoples could seek title to lands that they had not given up title to in the past, (2) resource-based industries could not impact aboriginal lands, and (3) Aboriginal Peoples could receive compensation for impacted lands. This decision by the Supreme Court, known as Delgamuukw, clearly defined aboriginal rights in British Columbia.

Another important ruling by the Supreme Court of Canada stated that the federal and provincial governments must consult Aboriginal Peoples about land development activities that could impact their rights and potential ownership of lands. This ruling protects the collective rights guaranteed to aboriginal groups by the Charter.

Additionally, in 1999, the Supreme Court ruled that Section 77 (1) of the Indian Act, which stated that only First Nations peoples who lived on reserves could vote in elections for band leaders, violated the Charter rights of First Nations peoples. John Corbiere, chief of Ontario's Batchewana Nation for many years, worked hard to change this legislation so that equity (fairness) would exist between First Nations peoples who lived on reserves and those who lived off reserves. He hoped that aboriginal community governments would improve as a result of this change.

PROTECTING COLLECTIVE RIGHTS FOR ENGLISH-SPEAKING AND FRENCH-SPEAKING LANGUAGE MINORITIES IN CANADA

In support of Canadian democratic principles, the government wanted to treat each official language fairly and equally. Presently, approximately 82% of all Canadians use French or English as their first language. The Charter ensures that all parliamentary business among government representatives or involving citizens be conducted in either language. The Charter also ensures equity in the rights of both English-speaking and French-speaking communities throughout Canada. Both English-speaking and French-speaking Canadians played major roles in the political negotiations that led to the founding of Canada as a country. Thus, the Charter protects the collective rights of English-speaking and French-speaking Canadians whose communities make up a minority of their provincial populations.

Today, Francophones living outside Québec and throughout the rest of Canada, mainly in Ontario, make up approximately 5% of Canada's population. Alternatively, there are thousands of English-speaking Canadians who live in Québec but form a minority in that province. Previous to the Charter, some legislation in provinces did not recognize minority language rights. For example, in 1977, Bill 101 was passed in Québec. This law stipulated that only French and not English could exist on outdoor business or commercial signs in the province. After the Charter was introduced in 1982, a new law was necessary in Québec to protect English minority language rights not recognized by Bill 101. In 1993, Bill 86 was passed which allowed smaller English lettering on commercial signs.

Practice Questions: 8, 9

6.1.3.3 How did the Treaty of La Grande Paix de Montréal address collective identity and collective rights?

THE TREATY OF LA GRANDE PAIX DE MONTREAL AND COLLECTIVE IDENTITY AND RIGHTS

Prior to European settlement, Canada was inhabited by many aboriginal communities. The Europeans were the first non-aboriginal people to settle permanently in Canada. Jacques Cartier established France's claim to the territory in 1534. French rulers, as well as other European leaders who were also interested in these lands, did not view the Aboriginal Peoples as having any claim to the lands at all.

French rulers were particularly attracted to the wealth that the fur trade in New France could generate. French fur-trading posts were set up throughout the areas now called Ontario and Québec. Furs were traded between the French and their allies the Ouendat and Algonquin at these outposts. The King of France was eager to protect French interests in the fur trade by creating a strong French colony in New France, one that would not easily be taken over by competing European countries such as Britain. The French government, therefore, sought to encourage settlement in New France because they felt the colony would become stronger with greater numbers of people living there.

One major problem facing settlement of the colony in New France was that the Ouendat and Algonquin nations were in an ongoing conflict with their First Nations enemies to the south, the Haudenosaunee. The Haudenosaunee nation was made up of the Seneca, Cauga, Onondaga, Oneida, and Mohawk cultures. The conflict threatened the settlement at Montréal and French control of the fur trade. Ongoing warfare continued even though the French had negotiated a number of treaties between their allies and the Haudenosaunee. These treaties were ultimately broken.

THE TREATY OF LA GRANDE PAIX DE MONTREAL

The Governor of New France at the time, Louis-Hector de Callière, knew that the only way to end the warfare was to have all of the First Nations groups agree to peace. He invited dozens of First Nations groups, both allies and enemies of the French, to meet in a large multicultural gathering to discuss a trading and treaty partnership. Approximately 1 300 representatives from about 40 different First Nations groups travelled to Montréal during the summer of 1701 to meet and take part in negotiations. These negotiations led to the signing of the Treaty of La Grande Paix de Montréal (The Great Peace of Montréal).

During the negotiations, all the First Nation representatives were warmly welcomed by the French. As discussions took place over the two weeks, the representatives treated each other with respect and listened intently while each spoke. Each of the First Nations groups had their own beliefs and point of view (collective identity), and each of the First Nations representatives was treated and respected as a unique culture whose opinions and input were greatly valued. In other words, their collective rights to be heard and respected were recognized. Although each of the First Nations groups was a unique culture, all of the representatives worked together using cooperation and compromise for the common good. Together, they believed in the principles of peace, respect, compromise, and agreement. Ensuring the collective rights of each nation and establishing equality among the nations were priorities during negotiations. A collective identity of diplomacy and peace emerged during the discussions and led to the successful signing of the treaty.

The main terms of the treaty reflected the collective rights and collective identity of the First Nation participants at La Grande Paix. Each of the main terms of the treaty was born from a belief in the common good and equal rights for all who attended. Each First Nations representative signed the treaty with a symbol that represented each culture. This demonstrated the collective identity of each Nation that signed the treaty. It also demonstrated the expectation of each Nation that, by signing the treaty, their collective rights would always be respected. A wampum representing the signed treaty was given to each representative by the French Governor as a gift to take home to their First Nation group.

Main Terms of the Treaty of La Grande Paix de Montréal	Collective Identity and/or Collective Rights Reflected by the Main Terms of the Treaty
All First Nations agreed to peace.	Reflected the collective identity of peaceful diplomacy that was practiced by each First Nations representative at La Grande Paix
All First Nations had the right to use hunting lands to the north and west of Lake Ontario.	Reflected the collective rights of each First Nations group represented at La Grande Paix
All First Nations agreed to take any future matters of disagreement to the French Governor rather than to declare war.	Reflected the collective identity of peaceful diplomacy that was practiced by each First Nations representative at La Grande Paix; also reflected that each Nation had collective rights to be respected and listened to in matters of dispute and to respect the rights of others

Practice Question: 10

6.1.3.4 How do the Treaty of La Grande Paix de Montréal and the Canadian Charter of Rights and Freedoms compare in the way each addresses individual and collective identity and collective rights?

THE TREATY OF LA GRANDE PAIX DE MONTREAL AND THE CANADIAN CHARTER OF RIGHTS AND FREEDOMS

The Treaty of La Grande Paix de Montréal (1701) and the Canadian Charter of Rights and Freedoms (1982) occurred nearly 300 years apart, yet there are strong similarities between the two documents in the way each addresses individual and collective identity and collective rights.

Individual Identity—During the weeks of negotiations that led to the Treaty of La Grande Paix de Montréal, the individual identity of each of the represented First Nations groups was highly respected. Each representative was listened to intently as they expressed the point of view of the First Nations group that they represented. Each representative was considered an equal with each other and with the French. The Charter of Rights and Freedoms, in comparison, respects and guarantees the individual rights and freedoms of all Canadian citizens. This is the law of the land.

Collective Identity—The Treaty of La Grande Paix respected the collective identity of all of the First Nations groups attending. It also recognized the French and First Nations as equal and independent nations. The Charter, in comparison, respects the collective identity of the Aboriginal Peoples of Canada. Today, the Charter also respects the collective identity of official language minority groups in Canada.

Collective Rights—The Treaty of La Grande Paix sought to ensure the collective rights of all First Nations groups that attended and those of the French. For the First Nations groups, these collective rights involved the ability to make their own decisions and to hunt on territorial lands. Today, the Charter guarantees to protect the collective rights of the Aboriginal Peoples of Canada and also official language minority groups in the country. Writing the Charter offered the Canadian government a chance to correct past injustices and offer Aboriginal Peoples the opportunity to seek self-government and manage their lands. With the Charter, treaty rights became entrenched in the Constitution.

The Treaty of La Grande Paix can be viewed as an early model of human rights in Canada. The treaty was created through the use of diplomacy by all who attended. It was built on principles of fairness, equality, respect, representation, and fundamental freedoms, all of which are principles that Canadian democracy of today and the Canadian Charter of Rights and Freedoms are built on. Presently, the Charter is the law of the land in Canada because it is entrenched in the Constitution of Canada. Just over 300 years ago, the Treaty of La Grande Paix de Montréal was also respected as the law of the land that the French and First Nations shared.

Practice Question: 11

6.1.3.5 Why is the Canadian Charter of Rights and Freedoms entrenched in the Canadian Constitution?

THE CANADIAN CHARTER OF RIGHTS AND FREEDOMS AND THE CANADIAN CONSTITUTION

The intent in creating the Charter was to protect a clearly defined list of democratic and constitutional rights and freedoms for all Canadian citizens. The Charter would guarantee a free and democratic society for all Canadians and future generations. Therefore, the Canadian government created the Canadian Charter of Rights and Freedoms, composed of 34 sections, to guarantee that several groups of individual rights and freedoms would always be protected and ensured for all Canadian citizens. Also, by having the individual rights and freedoms of Canadians stated in the Charter, citizens are protected from any future unjust government action that could occur. Thus, democracy will always be maintained in our country.

To make sure that the individual rights and freedoms of Canadians are protected to the greatest extent possible, the Charter was entrenched in the Constitution of Canada, our country's most supreme document. This occurred on April 17, 1982 (Constitution Act) during the patriation of Canada's Constitution. However, one section of the Charter (Section 15) did not come into effect for three years in order to give the provinces enough time to bring their equality laws into line with the Charter.

Because individual and collective rights and freedoms of Canadians are stated in the Charter and the Charter is entrenched in Canada's Constitution, these rights and freedoms became the law of Canada. They cannot be changed by the government and must always be protected and upheld. To change the rights of Canadians would require changing the Constitution, which would be difficult to do. Entrenching the Charter's rights and freedoms in the Constitution of Canada ensures that Canadians live in a free and democratic society.

Prior to the creation of the Charter, the individual rights of Canadians had been addressed in the Canadian Bill of Rights, passed in 1960. The Canadian Bill of Rights was an earlier human rights charter in Canada that addressed several rights and freedoms, but it was more limited for two reasons. In the first place, it could be changed because it was a bill. In the second place, it could not be used to interpret provincial laws, only federal laws. Unlike the Charter of Rights and Freedoms (1982), the Canadian Bill of Rights did not have provincial approval when it was passed in 1960.

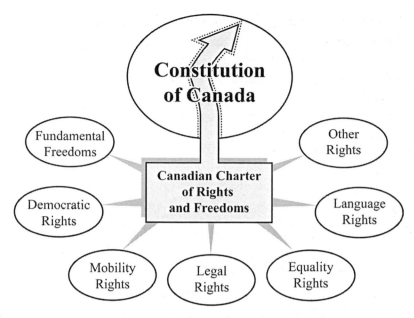

The Canadian Charter of Rights and Freedoms
is firmly entrenched in the Constitution of Canada.
Therefore, the democratic freedoms and rights
of Canadian citizens are protected and ensured
for future generations.

Practice Question: 12

6.1.4.1 How are representatives chosen to form a local government?

HOW REPRESENTATIVES FORM A LOCAL GOVERNMENT

Towns, cities, villages, summer villages, and municipal districts are all examples of municipalities. Each municipality in Alberta has its own form of local government. Local elections usually occur every three years. In these elections, citizens vote for a candidate to represent the particular area or community they live in. This process is referred to as the **electoral process.** The electoral process is an important part of our democratic system of government.

Local governments try to better understand the needs of the people by ensuring that candidates are local citizens themselves. In fact, any Canadian citizen who is 18 years of age or over and has lived in a municipality for at least six months can be nominated by eligible voters to be a candidate in a local election. One exception to this, however, is that residents of summer villages who have not lived in their community for six months can still run in an election as long as they are a property owner or are married to a property owner.

Cities and municipal districts are divided into geographic areas called wards. Wards are determined by the number of people living in an area. Candidates who run in elections in municipalities other than cities that have ward systems, must have lived in their own ward for at least six months prior to election day. Candidates in city elections must have lived within the city for at least six months prior to the election.

After candidates are nominated to run for office and pay a candidate's fee, they campaign. During the campaign, they make public speeches to let voters know what they stand for. They are often assisted by a campaign committee. An appointed returning officer and election officers are in charge of preparing lists of eligible voters and overseeing the electoral process. On election day, electors (voters) travel to local polling stations to mark their ballots with an "X" for the candidate of their choice. The candidates with the majority of votes win the election.

Local governments in municipalities may include both elected and appointed officials. The elected members of local governments are called council members. Councils are made up of the elected leader and the elected councillors. If a council member needs to resign before the next general election, a **by-election** is held to fill the vacant position.

The elected leader is called the **mayor** in urban areas or the **reeve** in rural areas. The mayor or reeve works with the councillors to govern the municipality, make decisions, and perform other official and ceremonial functions. Each council member represents the constituents who live in the area that they represent. The role of councillors include assisting the mayor in making decisions, discussing particular issues, developing programs and policies in municipalities, and creating and passing bylaws.

Although you are too young to vote in local elections, you can still influence local government to make a change if you feel something is in the best interest of the community. You can play a part in making a change that benefits the common good or supports the conservation of the environment in the following way.

An Example of How Students Can Take Part in Local Government

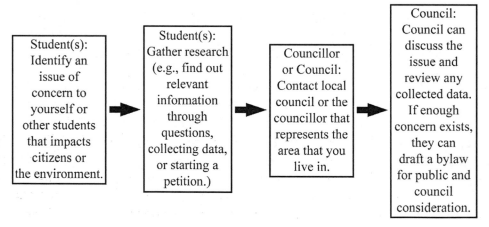

Student(s): Identify an issue of concern to yourself or other students that impacts citizens or the environment.

Student(s): Gather research (e.g., find out relevant information through questions, collecting data, or starting a petition.)

Councillor or Council: Contact local council or the councillor that represents the area that you live in.

Council: Council can discuss the issue and review any collected data. If enough concern exists, they can draft a bylaw for public and council consideration.

Practice Questions: 13, 14

6.1.4.2 What are the responsibilities of local governments?

THE RESPONSIBILITIES OF LOCAL GOVERNMENTS

Local governments, also called municipal governments, exist to democratically serve the needs of individuals and groups and to ensure the quality of life within their communities. Local governments in Alberta are very similar in the responsibilities they have toward citizens and the community. They differ, however, in the kinds of decisions they make and the issues they face. The reason for the difference is that governing factors are based on unique environments and the different resources available in each community. Local governments are responsible for promoting citizenship and the continued growth and sustainability of their environments. Sustainability refers to the responsible protection and conservation of local resources to ensure that there are resources available for future generations living in the community.

Local government has several main responsibilities which include the following:

- Ensuring that citizen's input is heard regarding needs within the community

- Enforcing local bylaws and passing new bylaws when necessary to resolve local issues and respond to citizens' needs

- Providing required services to the community

- Collecting taxes, the main source of revenue, to pay for the services provided

CITIZEN INPUT

Since local governments are created to democratically serve the needs of citizens, they try to listen to individual needs and concerns and give citizens the opportunity to express their opinions. Citizens are also offered the opportunity to take part in local government in a number of ways. Voting for representatives offers citizens the chance to personally select their choice of candidate to represent their needs. Also, citizens are encouraged to attend council meetings and express their views on issues and proposed changes. Citizens may also, if they wish, run for office themselves and participate in local government to an even greater degree. The level of one's involvement in local government is a personal choice, but all citizens are encouraged to actively become involved to some extent and to volunteer within their communities.

LOCAL ISSUES AND BYLAWS

There are a number of ways that local governments can resolve issues in their communities. For example, a local council can conduct a survey to find out what people think about an issue. They can also create and pass laws (called bylaws) and resolutions in their municipality that deal with ongoing problems and concerns.

The Municipal Government Act states that local councils can pass bylaws that concern the following matters:

- Safety and protection of citizens and property

- Issues concerning public places

- Nuisances (e.g., property that is not cared for or is unsightly)

- Business activities

- Transportation systems

- Municipal services

- Public utilities

- Animals and their related activities

- Bylaw enforcement

Bylaws are rules that guide people's behaviour within a community in order to protect the safety and respect the rights of all citizens living there. As such, bylaws are only enforced in areas where they are passed. The penalty for breaking a bylaw is usually a fine.

Bylaws are usually introduced by local government councillors who make a motion for a bylaw to be made or changed from its present form in order to better meet the needs of the citizens living within the community. Citizens can also request a town council or city council to pass a bylaw. Bylaws are discussed and considered three times by local government members, and public input is welcomed at these times. Each bylaw is then voted on by councilors. A majority vote is necessary for a bylaw to be passed or changed. During this process of creating bylaws, citizens are involved in the democratic process.

There are many, many bylaws that exist to control the activities of citizens in a community. Setting a curfew time for teenagers, banning the ownership of certain breeds of dogs, placing cats on a leash, and allowing parking on only one side of the street are all bylaws that exist in some Canadian cities. Bylaws are created to make the community a pleasant and safe place for all citizens and to address important environmental issues.

Many newly passed and proposed bylaws address environmental issues in municipal areas. For example, in January of 2009 following public consultation with citizens, a city anti-idling bylaw was drafted. It was then presented for discussion and debate by a city council committee in Edmonton. This law, if passed, will limit the amount of time allowed for the stationary idling of vehicles to just a few minutes. For example, if your parent was parked in the car in front of the school, the engine could only be run for a minute or two. If more time was required to wait for you, the engine would have to be turned off. The fine for not obeying the bylaw is proposed to be hundreds of dollars. The intent of this proposed bylaw is to cut down on fuel emissions. By doing this, we would protect the quality of the air in our city and promote the sustainability of our environment for generations to come.

Some older and historic bylaws that were passed in Canada are somewhat humourous in this day and age. In at least one Canadian community, it is illegal to climb trees. In another, it is illegal to have a horse stand on the street for more than a few minutes. In the 1970s, a Canadian television program called *This is the Law* involved a panel that tried to guess what old law or bylaw in Canada was being broken during brief but humourously presented film clips.

SERVICES

Canadian democracy ensures that local governments provide citizens with some of the services that are necessary for their quality of life. Local governments provide services in many of the following areas:

- daycare centres
- seniors' facilities
- libraries
- parks
- recreational facilities and programs
- road construction and bridge-building
- public transportation
- emergency medical and disaster services
- firefighting services
- police services
- garbage collection and disposal
- land and housing
- storm sewers and drainage
- water treatment and supply
- various other local services

TAXES AND OTHER REVENUE SOURCES

Local governments require money to provide services, to resolve local issues, and to respond to community needs. The most common way for local goverments to gain revenue (income) is through the collection of property taxes. Taxes are basically fees assigned annually to property owners on their businesses, houses, and property. Only governments can collect taxes. They use the funds they collect to provide the needed services to the people.

Taxes pay for a number of services within a community that local government is responsible for. However, the revenue needed by local governments to provide services must also come from other sources. Some of these sources include funds received from the federal or provincial levels of government, from user fees, and from monies raised from community equipment rental. Here are two examples of cases in which the government does not pay for the complete service.

Example 1: A local government may maintain an arena with monies raised by taxes, but citizens may pay a fee to skate in the arena. This fee provides a portion of the money necessary to maintain the arena for the use of the community.

Example 2: Power consumption and water supply are paid for by home and business-owners within communities. The government is only responsible for making sure that utilities such as electricity and water are available for people to purchase. People need to pay the cost of electricity and water consumption themselves.

When not enough revenue is generated for the costs of municipal government services, there are sometimes tax increases assigned to property owners to pay for the shortfall. User fees may also have to be increased so citizens can receive a number of necessary services that are not designated as a local government responsibility.

Practice Questions: 15, 16

6.1.4.3 How are local governments structured differently in rural and urban settings?

LOCAL GOVERNMENTS IN RURAL AND URBAN SETTINGS

Municipalities contain the population of people living within designated boundaries. Although municipalities may be referred to as urban or rural settings, many municipalities contain ways of life that are both urban and rural in nature.

Municipalities in Alberta

Local governments exist in all municipalities, regardless of size. The purpose of all local governments is to govern communities effectively, to provide services and facilities to citizens that live there, to provide safe environments, and to ensure the growth and sustainability of the community. In some cases, when municipalities have not been able to meet the needs of residents, specialized municipalities have been formed. This usually happens because of unique circumstances in those particular areas. Specialized municipalities may be both urban and rural in nature. The municipalities of Jasper and Strathcona County are both examples of specialized municipalities in Alberta.

URBAN AND RURAL SETTINGS FOR LOCAL GOVERNMENT IN ALBERTA

Urban Settings support larger population bases and include:

- Larger urban municipalities (e.g., cities)

- Smaller urban municipalities (e.g., towns, villages)

Rural Settings have lower populations and vary in rural geography (i.e., parkland, forested areas, farmland) and include:

- Municipal districts (include counties and other rural areas such as hamlets and residential subdivisions in the countryside)

- Métis settlements

- First Nations reserves

FIRST NATIONS AND MÉTIS FORMS OF LOCAL GOVERNMENT

First Nations

First Nations reserves are not a part of any municipalities. According to the British North America Act of 1867, the federal government assumed and maintains legislative authority and responsibility for First Nations reserves. However, each First Nation community in Alberta has its own local form of self-government called a band council. This council includes an elected chief and an appointed council. The larger the population a First Nations community has, the greater the number of councillors that represent the citizens living there. Bylaws in each community, known as Band Council Resolutions, are passed by the chief and councillors.

The Métis

The Métis also have their own form of local self-government. In 1991, Alberta became the first province to pass specific legislation for the Métis people. This legislation was developed by the Métis people and the Alberta government working together. Its purpose was to help the Métis secure and control their own lands and to develop independence and autonomy in self-governing their settlement communities. Presently, there are 9 000 people who live on eight Métis settlements in Alberta. These settlements are located at Peavine, Kikino, Paddle River, Elizabeth, East Prairie, Gift Lake, Paddle Prairie, and Fishing Lake. Each of the eight Métis settlements is governed by a five-member local council that is elected every three years and a chairperson selected by the councillors from among themselves. Local councils govern local areas and make bylaws for their communities. All of the combined 40 councillors from the local councils make up the Métis Settlements General Council, which politically oversees all of the Métis living in all eight settlements.

Structure of Métis Local Government in Alberta

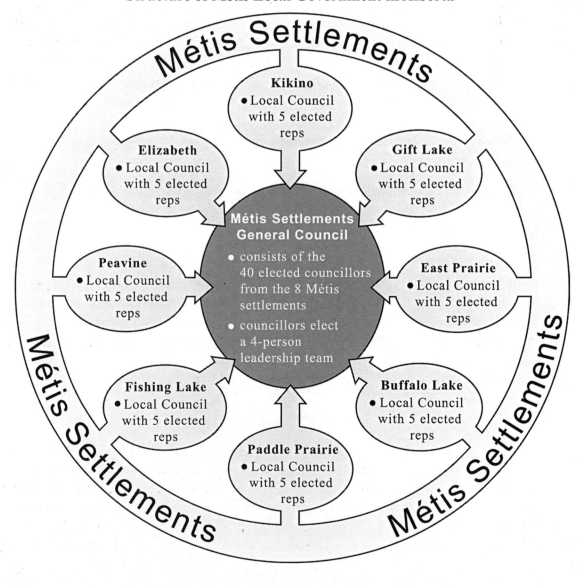

COMPARING SIMILARITIES AND DIFFERENCES BETWEEN RURAL AND URBAN LOCAL GOVERNMENT

Similarities and Differences

The structure of urban and rural local governments in Alberta are quite similar. The differences occur mainly because of the larger numbers of citizens being served in urban communities and the differing geographic environments.

Urban local governments and rural local governments both have the following structures:

- **An elected council**—The elected council consists of a leader called a mayor (in urban settings) or a reeve (in rural settings) and councillors (7 to 15 councillors in urban settings and fewer in rural settings).

- **Committees and a chief administrative officer** (also known as the town or city manager)— The elected council in both urban and rural forms of local government work closely with council committees (elected and hired individuals), advisory committees (elected, hired, or volunteers), and the chief administrative officer, who is appointed. The chief administrative officer plays a very important role communicating information to the elected council about how the municipalities are operating so that council can make informed decisions. It is his or her duty to ensure that local government responsibilities are carried out.

- **Departments** (e.g., planning and development, public works, parks and recreation)— These are areas that provide municipal services and report their daily operations to the town or city manager. Departments are run by hired individuals called civil servants. Departments in urban settings and rural settings sometimes differ because of the surrounding environments. For example, an agricultural services department is more likely to be found in a rural local government setting than an urban setting.

Generally, as urban areas have greater numbers of people living there, there will be more councillors elected. Also, greater numbers of government department employees will be hired to serve the larger number of citizens. This is a result of the size of the population base being served.

Practice Question: 17

6.1.4.4 What role is played by school boards within local communities?

THE ROLE OF SCHOOL BOARDS IN LOCAL COMMUNITIES

The province of Alberta is responsible for Alberta's education. However, it is the role of local school boards throughout the province to provide education to meet the educational needs within their particular urban or rural community. Think of school boards as a kind of local government that governs education. Presently in Alberta, there are more than 50 different school boards, including public, separate, private, and Francophone. School boards have elections for their leaders, just like local government. In fact, there may be several different school boards within a municipality.

You might like to find out what school board has authority over your school, your friends' schools, or your relatives' schools. School boards are actually just one example of existing special boards or councils in Alberta that have governing powers and are called local authorities. For example, health boards or councils that commonly exist in municipalities throughout Alberta are also referred to as local authorities.

School boards govern by developing policies and making decisions about local education. A school board leadership team, made up of a hired superintendent and elected trustees, makes decisions on matters of policy, educational programming, and services for schools throughout their local areas. The trustees are elected every three years at the same time as local government elections. Alberta's School Act provides that First Nations communities located near school districts are able to nominate a First Nations representative to serve on school boards and be assigned the same responsibilities and duties as other board members.

The superintendent of a school board has the role of being responsible for the entire school board, its budget, and the operation of all the board's schools. The trustees assist the superintendent by making decisions about budget expenditures, educational programs, student transportation, and the curriculum. They also make rules for schools and listen to and address any concerns from parents and concerned citizens.

Education in Alberta

An important principle that Alberta's education system maintains is the freedom of the parents to choose the type of school that their children attend. There are numerous school settings for children in Alberta, and a number of children are home-schooled. Regardless of the setting, the educational curriculum that is taught is stipulated by the provincial government and closely followed by school boards and other education providers. For example, you are currently studying the Grade 6 social studies curriculum about the democratic process in Alberta. Your student peers in other school settings in Alberta will most likely be studying similar topics during the course of their school year.

Schools in Alberta

Many different types of schools exist in Alberta. The following list describes the main types you will find:

Separate Schools

Most schools run by separate school boards in Alberta follow the Roman Catholic faith in school programming. They also offer a wide range of instructional subjects and follow the provincial curriculum. Although there are some exceptions, the majority of separate schools in Alberta are Catholic.

Public Schools

The schools run by public boards are generally open to all students living in the community. The majority of these schools offer classes in the English language. However, a number of public schools are French Immersion (where French is the language in which classes are taught) or schools that offer bilingual programs. In bilingual programs, English is used to instruct students part of the time and another specified language, such as Chinese, Japanese, German, or Ukrainian, is used to instruct students the rest of the time.

Francophone Schools

The Canadian Charter of Rights and Freedoms protects the collective rights of French-speaking Albertans whose communities make up a minority of the population in our province. This means that Francophone parents have the right to have Francophone schools teach their children in places where there are enough Francophone students to require it. They also have the right to have Francophone school boards run and oversee those schools. Therefore, all Francophone schools are the responsibility of Francophone school boards in Alberta, with the exception of private schools.

First Nation, Métis, and Inuit Schools / Educational Programming

In our province, Alberta Education works together with First Nations, Métis, and Inuit (FNMI) community elders, educators, and parents to learn the best ways to serve the needs of FNMI students and blend FNMI perspectives into the Alberta curriculum. Many First Nations and Métis settlement schools exist in our province. The schools incorporate an aboriginal perspective into school programming and celebrate aboriginal identity and culture. Language instruction is provided in First Nations schools in Blackfoot or Cree. For example, Cree is studied at the Ermineskin Schools that are located on the Ermineskin Cree Reserve. The Caslan School is an example of a Métis settlement school. Located at Caslan, near the Buffalo Lake Métis Settlement, the school educates Métis children from the settlement and celebrates Métis identity and culture through the school's programming, which includes Métis art and dance. Student dancers from the Caslan School have performed Métis dances for audiences locally and in British Columbia.

A number of Alberta's public school systems offer programs taught from a FNMI perspective. For example, the Medicine Wheel Kindergarten Program, which is located in Harold W. Riley School in Calgary's public school system, provides education to Métis students. Edmonton Public School System offers the Awasis Program, which enables students to learn about and increase their appreciation and knowledge of aboriginal traditions and cultures. Many other schools in Alberta's public school systems also offer courses in aboriginal studies or aboriginal languages.

Charter Schools

A number of charter schools have been built in Alberta. Charter schools have often been formed to provide enhanced educational programming to a particular group of students. Although charter schools provide the same provincial curriculum as other schools in Alberta, there are particular characteristics that differentiate charter schools from the public school system. For example, charter schools often have specific programming, teaching approaches, and a focus on a particular area of study, like religion, fine arts, or athletics. Local school boards do not govern charter schools.

Private Schools

The provincial government has long recognized that parents can educate their children outside the public school system. Therefore, a number of children attend private schools in Alberta. Tuition and fees are usually charged by private schools. Since 1969, the Government of Alberta has provided financial support to private schools. A wide variety of private schools exist in the province.

Practice Question: 18

6.1.5.1 How is the provincial government structured?

THE STRUCTURE OF THE PROVINCIAL GOVERNMENT

The members of our provincial government meet at the Alberta Legislature Building, which is located in Edmonton. Every year, hundreds of school children from throughout Alberta take part in school tours at the Legislature Building.

In the provincial government of Alberta, the political party with the most members of the legislative assembly (MLAs) elected in a provincial election governs the province. Their leader becomes the Premier. It is the duty of the lieutenant-governor, as Chief Executive Officer of the province of Alberta and as the Queen's representative, to ensure that the position of Premier is always filled.

Each MLA is elected by citizens in a constituency (voting district) to represent their constituency in the legislative assembly and to work in different government activities, such as creating laws. The legislative assembly is the law-making branch of government. There are 83 MLAs elected in Alberta's provincial elections. Each MLA represents one constituency in the province. The boundaries of Alberta's constituencies are determined by population, geography, and other factors.

Not all MLAs elected to the legislative assembly are from the same political party. There are a number of MLAs elected who are from other political parties than the party in power. Those MLAs are called the Opposition. Like all MLAs, Opposition members serve in the legislative assembly to represent the citizens of the constituency in which they were elected. Opposition members analyze and question government plans, initiatives, and activities. They also provide alternatives and recommend improvements.

Following an election, the Premier selects a number of MLAs from his own political party to serve in his cabinet as cabinet ministers. The Premier assigns a different area of responsibility to each cabinet minister. This means that each cabinet minister oversees the services of a particular government department. The Premier is responsible for international and intergovernmental relations.

The Premier and the cabinet together form the executive council. Cabinet ministers support and work with the Premier to make decisions, develop government policies, and plan appropriate government spending and actions.

Each government department provides services to the citizens of Alberta. Departments employ civil servants to look after the everyday running of the department.

Practice Question: 19

6.1.5.2 What is the role and status of the lieutenant-governor within the provincial government?

THE ROLE AND STATUS OF THE LIEUTENANT-GOVERNOR

According to the British North America Act of 1867, lieutenant-governors are to act on behalf of the Queen and be her representative in Canada. When the province of Alberta was created in 1905, the office of the lieutenant-governor of Alberta was established. At one time, the lieutenant-governor was also considered an agent of the federal government and was expected to advise the Alberta government in matters of federal legislation to make sure that provincial laws are in agreement with federal laws.

Over time, provincial governments developed more authority and the lieutenant-governor no longer needed to advise the government about the agreement of provincial and federal laws. The lieutenant-governor's role and status became specifically that of Chief Executive Officer of the province of Alberta and the Queen's representative in Alberta. Although Canada is a fully independent country, it remains, by choice, a member country of the British Commonwealth. Since the Queen is the Head of the Commonwealth, the lieutenant-governor represents Her Majesty the Queen in the province of Alberta. As the Queen's representative, the lieutenant-governor is regarded and addressed with the highest respect and honour.

The lieutenant-governor is always referred to directly as "Your Honour" and to others as "His Honour" or "the Lieutenant-Governor." The spouse of a lieutenant-governor is referred to as His or Her Honour.

The office of the lieutenant-governor is a permanent position in Alberta's provincial government because,

> "The Offices of the Monarch, Governor General, and Lieutenant Governor are entrenched in the Canadian Constitution, and no changes can be made to the Offices without the unanimous approval of all Provincial Legislative Assemblies, and the Senate, and the House of Commons in Ottawa."
>
> —*from* http://www.lieutenantgovernor.ab.ca/index

The lieutenant-governor is appointed by the Governor General of Canada upon recommendation of the Prime Minister. The role of the lieutenant-governor is one that has long been associated with Alberta's history, heritage, and traditions. In fact, in addition to the lieutenant-governor's constitutional role as the Queen's representative, the office of the lieutenant-governor assists in preserving Alberta's traditions and character. The lieutenant-governor does not show favouritism toward the members or policies of any political party, nor does the lieutenant-governor belong to a political party.

The lieutenant-governor has three main types of duties: (1) constitutional, (2) social, and (3) ceremonial.

The constitutional duties of the lieutenant-governor include the following:

- Granting royal assent to all of the bills that are passed by MLAs in the legislative assembly. In other words, he or she must approve of each bill and sign it in order for it to become the law in Alberta. There are also a number of other documents and proclamations that the lieutenant-governor signs to make them official

- Summoning and ending sessions of the legislature

- Reading the speech from the throne during the opening of each legislature session

- Dissolving (ending) the legislature session before an election

- Being responsible to see that the role of premier is always filled

- Presiding over the swearing-in of the new members in the premier's cabinet

The social duties of the lieutenant-governor include the following:

- Attending government ceremonies on behalf of the Queen

- Attending social events

- Meeting and conversing with Albertans whenever possible

The ceremonial duties of the lieutenant-governor include the following:

• Taking part in awards ceremonies

• Presenting awards to Albertans who have made notable contributions

The lieutenant-governor presides over the Alberta Order of Excellence Awards. This award, which recognizes a citizen's lifetime of work and service to the community, is the highest award and honour that Alberta citizens can achieve. Additionally, the lieutenant-governor is the Chair of the Duke of Edinburgh Awards. These awards are presented to young Albertans aged 14 to 25 who set and achieve personal goals in four areas: skills, physical recreation, adventurous journey, and community service. The intent of these awards is to help young people develop responsibility by actively taking part in activities, interests, and volunteerism. Since the awards were started in 1954, nearly 6 000 000 young people in 120 countries around the world have taken part in the challenge of the Duke of Edinburgh Awards.

Albertans have benefitted greatly from the many contributions made to our province and communities by Alberta's lieutenant-governors. Our most recent lieutenant-governor, the Honourable Norman L. Kwong, became our 16th lieutenant-governor in 2005. He has just completed his term, and his contributions to the province are valued by the people of Alberta.

Lt.-Gov. Kwong grew up in Calgary, the son of Chinese immigrants Lily and Charles Kwong. While attending Western Canada High School in Calgary, he developed a love of and a talent for football. At the age of 18, he started a professional sporting career. He won Grey Cup football honours and set 30 records during a very successful career as a player. Later, he was successful as a manager. His Honour again received top honours as a co-owner of the Calgary Flames when they won the Stanley Cup in 1989. Lt.-Gov. Kwong also had a very successful professional career in real estate.

Lt.-Gov. Kwong has received many awards of distinction in various areas. His Honour has exemplified citizenship and volunteerism to all citizens in our province. In 1998, His Honour became a Member of the Order of Canada. In 2005, he received the Alberta Order of Excellence and was knighted the Order of St. John of Jerusalem by the Queen. Family is very important to His Honour, and he has been married for 49 years. He has four sons and eight grandchildren.

Although he was involved in many activities throughout the province, His Honour established four areas that he wanted to focus on during his service in office. He wanted to encourage Albertans to establish and maintain a balanced, healthy lifestyle, support multicultural endeavours, champion seniors' involvement within their communities, and promote citizenship among all Albertans. The following statements are comments that he made about these four areas of focus during his welcome address to the citizens of Alberta.

Balanced Living: "I strongly believe that a healthy and balanced lifestyle is key to living a rich and full life. Daily activity is something we can all do...the trick is to find something that you love to do...My own involvement in amateur and professional sports brought huge benefits to my personal and professional life; I learned self-confidence, discipline, responsibility, and the value of friendships..."

Multiculturalism: "Growing up as a member of a visible minority, I understand the challenges faced by immigrants, particularly immigrant youth. I believe that we all have a lot to gain from sharing our stories and perspectives and I am encouraged by the work taking place across Alberta to build bridges of understanding between peoples of different cultures and philosophies."

Seniors: "...It's important for seniors to remain as physically, mentally, and socially active as possible. No matter our age, we have something special to contribute."

Citizenship: "...I have been working to promote young Albertan's awareness of the role of Lieutenant Governors in Canada's system of government...and to encourage our youngest citizens to be active and engaged members of their communities."

Practice Question: 20

6.1.5.3 What are the responsibilities of the provincial government?

THE RESPONSIBILITIES OF THE PROVINCIAL GOVERNMENT

The provincial government of Alberta is responsible to democratically serve the needs and interests of all the citizens of the province. The legislative assembly is responsible for making laws, collecting taxes, providing services and programs for Albertans, developing economic initiatives, and safeguarding environmental sustainability to help Alberta grow and be viable for generations to come.

THE FIVE PRIORITIES OF THE GOVERNMENT OF ALBERTA

The Government of Alberta has identified five priorities to work toward in order to make Alberta an even better and stronger province for today and for future generations. The government's five priorities that guide its work are to:

- Create opportunities to build the Alberta economy

- Improve the health care system in our province to better serve citizens' needs

- Build and plan for tomorrow by spending wisely and maintaining current hospitals, schools, and roads while also planning for new ones

- Develop the province's resources while also protecting the sustainability of our natural environment

- Shape strong communities that are vibrant and safe places for citizens to live, and provide citizens with access to culture and the arts

LAWS

Members of the legislative assembly (MLAs) have been elected by constituencies to represent citizens and to work in the many areas of government. This work includes the creation of laws that benefit the citizens of Alberta and the environment. MLAs make laws for the common good of all citizens. Albertans are then responsible to obey these laws. An MLA who helps create a law that citizens do not care for may not get re-elected in a future provincial election. This is an example of the dynamic relationship that exists between government and citizens as they take part in the democratic process.

Before a law is passed, it is originally introduced as a **bill** (proposed law) by an MLA and a **first reading** takes place in the Legislative Assembly.

At this point, the bill is studied and public input about the proposed bill is welcomed, e.g., at public meetings, through petitions, and letters.

Next, a second reading of the bill takes place in the Legislative Assembly, followed by debate by MLAs over the bill, and then a vote. If the bill is supported by the majority of MLAs, it will then be sent to a committee for study and any possible changes or revision.

Finally, if the bill has not been defeated to this point, a third reading of the bill takes place in the Legislative Assembly. Discussion, questions, or debate over the bill may also occur. Again, the bill is voted on by MLAs and if the majority of MLAs support the bill, it officially becomes an act (law) after it is signed by the Lieutenant Governor of Alberta.

SERVICES

The provincial government provides services to Albertans that are necessary and that enhance their quality of life. There are more than 20 government departments that provide specific services to Albertans. A cabinet minister is responsible for each of the departments.

Here is a list of all government of Alberta departments. Each department provides a variety of services to Albertans:

- Advanced Education and Technology
- Education
- Energy
- Finance
- Health and Wellness
- Treasury
- Environment
- Transportation
- Aboriginal Relations
- Justice and Attorney General
- Agriculture and Rural Development
- Children and Youth Services
- Seniors and Community Supports
- Employment and Immigration
- Sustainable Resource Development
- Solicitor General and Public Security
- Municipal Affairs
- Infrastructure
- Housing and Urban Affairs
- Culture and Community Spirit
- Tourism, Parks, and Recreation
- Service Alberta

Other levels of government (local and federal) also provide services that may overlap in some areas with the services provided by the provincial government. For example, roads are a responsibility of all three levels of government. During the spring of 2009, announcements were made stating that the governments of Canada and Alberta were investing millions of dollars in a number of Edmonton and Calgary transit projects. This initiative seeks to reduce greenhouse emissions, remove traffic congestion, and keep the cities safer.

TAXES

Services require funds to pay for them. Just as local governments collect taxes, the provincial government also collects taxes from citizens to cover the cost of services.

The right to health care and public education are important rights that are protected by the Alberta government. Approximately one-quarter of Alberta's tax dollars go toward education. Health services, followed by education services and social services receive the greatest amount of tax revenue collected in our province.

EXAMPLES OF NEW INITIATIVES

The Alberta government continually supports initiatives that enhance the quality of life in the province. The following are examples of some of the new political initiatives happening in our province.

Example 1

In the face of the recent global recession, the Alberta government seeks to acquire new markets, attract economic investment, and develop economic sustainability in Alberta.
Our government is seeking to market the Alberta story, and promote information about our resources, our strong fiscal position, and our low level of taxes and create strong economic interest from other world markets. Additionally, Alberta's new brand initiative seeks to attract the talent, investors, and tourists that can help the Alberta economy while at the same time supporting and promoting the sale of Alberta's goods and services abroad. With Alberta's new brand initiative, which the government considers to also be a tool that companies, organizations, and the government can use, Alberta's citizens and companies alike are considered ambassadors to promote Alberta and to spread the word of Alberta's new brand.

Example 2

Environmentally, the government seeks to protect the sustainability of Alberta's natural environment through a number of endeavors. Presently, the Alberta government is supporting the work of a research team seeking to reduce the use of natural gas and water during oil sands extraction work. The team is also investigating new processes that can protect the province's water supply during energy production. Of this new research, Doug Horner, the Minister of Advanced Education and Technology stated, "This investment in biotechnology research for energy production could result in new knowledge leading to billions of dollars in greener energy production." (quote taken from Government of Alberta News release, "Taking a natural path to greener energy production" May 20, 2009, http://alberta.ca/home/NewsFrame.cfm)

Practice Questions: 21, 22, 23

6.1.5.4 How are representatives chosen at the provincial level of government?

HOW ARE REPRESENTATIVES CHOSEN AT THE PROVINCIAL LEVEL OF GOVERNMENT?

The election process in Canada is similar for all levels of government. Candidates who run in Alberta provincial elections usually represent a particular political party, although some candidates run as independents. Political parties differ from each other in the political viewpoints, strategies, and policies that their party candidates represent.

The Premier and the MLAs are elected in their constituencies in provincial elections that are held every four years or so. The Canadian Charter of Rights and Freedoms states that the provincial government must call an election at least once every five years.

Each political party determines a candidate for their party before a provincial election is called. Usually, a nomination meeting produces the names of citizens interested in being the party candidate. A vote from within the party membership determines the candidate.

Each candidate in a provincial election must be eligible to vote themselves and must have an Elections Alberta form signed by 25 voters in their constituency. During the campaign, candidates spread the word about their ideas and what they will do for constituents and their community if elected. Candidates often have a campaign manager and workers to help with the campaign. All candidates may take part in debates with their opponents, but candidates for Premier are most likely to do so. Interested citizens watch the debates on television. Many candidates have had a surge of popularity following their participation in televised debates, often at the expense of their opponents.

On Election Day, eligible voters travel to the polls and mark a ballot with the letter "X" for the candidate they choose. The Chief Electoral Officer has the duty to ensure that the election proceeds smoothly and is run in a fair and professional manner. Albertans are eligible to vote if they are a Canadian citizen of 18 years of age or older, have a residence in the constituency in which they are voting, and have lived in Alberta for at least six months. Although elections are well publicized, many Albertans do not vote. This is not a scenario unique to Alberta, and many provinces advertise to increase voter turnout.

Alberta is organized into 83 voting districts that are called constituencies. During an election, one MLA is elected from each of the constituencies. The Premier must also be elected as the representative from his or her own constituency. It is the responsibility of each elected candidate to represent and serve the people who live within their particular constituency.

Alberta Provincial Election Results 1989–2008
Number of Candidates Elected from Each Political Party

Political Party	1989	1993	1997	2001	2004	2008
Progressive Conservative	59**	51**	63**	74**	62**	72**
Liberal	8	32*	18*	7*	16*	9*
New Democratic Party	16*	0	2	2	4	2
Alberta Alliance (2004) Wildrose Alliance (2008)	------	------	------	------	1	0
Other Parties & Independent Candidates	0	0	0	0	0	0
Total Seats	83	83	83	83	83	83

**denotes the political party that won the election
*denotes the political party that formed the official opposition

The given chart presents provincial political party election results in Alberta over nearly the last twenty years. Scan over the numbers. Do you see a trend here? The Progressive Conservative Party has been in power in Alberta since 1971, and the Liberal Party has formed the Official Opposition Party in Alberta since 1993.

Number of Elected Candidates of Each Political Party versus the Popular Vote of Albertans

Have you ever wondered if the total number of candidates of a political party elected in a provincial election actually reflects the number of Albertans who voted for that political party?

For instance, in the 2008 election, 72 out of 83 MLAs elected were from the Progressive Conservative Party. If you calculate 72 out of 83, you will find it equals 86.75%. Therefore, you know that 86.75% of the elected MLAs in 2008 were from the Progressive Conservative Party.

But does that mean that 86.75% of Albertans voted for Progressive Conservative Party candidates during the election? Take a closer look at the results of the 2008 provincial election in the given chart that compares the number of candidates elected from each political party to the popular vote of Albertans:

Results of the 2008 Alberta Provincial Election

Political Party	Number of MLAs Elected	% of MLAs Elected	Share of the Total Votes Cast in the Election
Progressive Conservative Party	72	86.75%	52.66%
Liberal Party	9	10.84%	26.37%
New Democratic Party	2	2.41%	8.52%
Wildrose Alliance Party	0	0%	6.77%
Green Party	0	0%	4.58%
Other Parties	0	0%	1.11%

What do these results demonstrate to you? Why would the Progressive Conservative Party have experienced such a solid victory (72 out of 83 seats won) and yet only have received 52.66% of the total votes that Albertans cast in the election? A couple of hypotheses (educated assumptions) can be made: a number of the constituencies may have experienced higher voter turnouts, and some constituencies may have had very close electoral races that could have seen other political parties than the Progressive Conservatives win those seats. For example, the Wildrose Alliance Party had some close results with other political parties yet did not win one MLA position in government (in one constituency, a Progressive Conservative candidate defeated the Wildrose Alliance candidate by only 36 votes). In actuality, just over half of Albertans voted for Progressive Conservative Party candidates in the last election though they won nearly 87% of the elected MLA positions.

Practice Question: 24

6.1.5.5 What are the differences between the responsibilities of a Member of the Legislative Assembly (MLA) and a cabinet minister?

RESPONSIBILITIES OF MEMBERS OF THE LEGISLATIVE ASSEMBLY

All MLAs have two main responsibilities:

First, MLAs need to represent the citizens of the constituency that elected them and be responsible for their political needs. In order to do this, they need to be actively involved in their constituency. This involves maintaining a public office in the constituency where they can meet with their constituents and hear their points of view or opinions on matters. MLAs also attend functions in their constituency. They keep constituents informed through newsletters and other forms of communication about government proposals, policies, activities, and programs. MLAs try to resolve any problems or issues that citizens may have with a government-related matter. You can think of an MLA as providing a link between his or her constituents and the provincial government.

It is an important principle of representative government for MLAs to represent the viewpoint of the majority of their constituents in government matters. MLAs also need to attend to the concerns of those in their constituency who may present alternative points of view. Opposition MLAs who support government initiatives and bills that are unpopular with the majority of their own constituents could possibly find themselves being voted out in the following election. Such is the unique relationship between citizens and government representatives in our democratic system of government in Canada.

Second, another main responsibility of MLAs is to participate in the many aspects of government. This may mean being actively involved in a number of government activities and working with other MLAs. One of these responsibilities involves the creation and introduction of bills. MLAs are involved in the study, discussion, and debate on bills. They are the ones who vote on whether to pass a bill or not.

MLAs also take part in other areas of government activity. They spend many hours working on committees. They study issues such as proposed bills and the need for programs and funding or services in different parts of the province. MLAs also work with special interest groups that might focus on need within the areas of education or the environment. MLAs take the concerns of citizens from within their own constituencies to the appropriate government ministry (department) so that those areas of need can be addressed and discussed.

RESPONSIBILITIES OF CABINET MINISTERS

Cabinet Ministers are MLAs who have been selected by the Premier to work with him. They help make decisions, develop government policies, review government spending, consider new laws, and plan initiatives, strategies, and actions that the government can take in order to respond to the needs of Albertans. The Premier and the Cabinet together form the **executive council.** Additionally, the Premier assigns each cabinet minister a different area of responsibility. This means that each cabinet minister has the responsibility of overseeing a particular government department.

Cabinet ministers have additional responsibilities beyond that of serving as an MLA for the citizens of the constituency that elected them. Cabinet ministers' extra responsibilities are (a) running their assigned department including the supervision of their department budget and overseeing the services and programs provided, (b) meeting with the Premier on political matters that affect the province of Alberta and developing plans of action that better serve the citizens of our province, and (c) overseeing committees and initiatives involving matters related to their own department. For example, one of the initiatives that the Alberta government's Ministry of Education is presently involved in is *Setting the Direction for Special Education in our Province*. Presently, a steering committee is gathering information and ideas from the public, parents, educators, and former students through questionnaires and public meetings to design a new framework that will best meet students' needs for special education in the province.

Practice Questions: 25

6.1.6.1 How can individuals, groups, and associations within a community participate in the decision-making process regarding current events or issues? (i.e., lobbying, petitioning, organizing and attending local meetings and rallies, contacting elected representatives).

PARTICIPATING IN THE DECISION-MAKING PROCESS

There are many ways that individuals, groups, and associations can take part in the decision-making process in their communities regarding important issues or current event matters. In fact, the functioning and success of our democratic system of government depends on everyone participating in the decision-making process. Individuals, groups, and associations can make valuable contributions toward improving conditions in local communities and in other needy parts of the world as well.

Over the years, there have been many changes in the way we do things in our communities. Our governments have created new bylaws, started new programs, and provided more services. These changes have improved the common good and met the needs of all the citizens in communities across Canada. Many of these changes occurred after an individual or group of citizens brought a concern about a particular issue to the attention of a government representative. Consequently, the issue was studied over time and action was taken. Indeed, many changes have originated from the participation and efforts of individual citizens or groups of citizens working with government members. Some changes have involved building ramps into public buildings for access by disabled citizens, changing speed zones by creating bylaws that better serve the safety of citizens, and protecting our natural habitats and the animals that make their homes there.

Citizens can take part in the decision-making process in other ways as well. They can contact council members at the local level of government and speak directly to them about a concern. At the provincial level, they can address their concerns to their member of the legislative assembly (MLA). At the federal level, they may contact their member of Parliament (MP). The Charter of Rights and Freedoms gives Canadians the right to express their opinions, to work together with others, to take a peaceful form of action, and to achieve a solution to a common concern or issue. Individuals, groups, and associations can also write letters to the editors of local newspapers to share their concerns or points of view. Some people organize and participate in public rallies or peaceful demonstrations to show how they feel about issues. Other groups raise funds or create public awareness for their cause in other ways.

Many citizens participate in government by voting for government representatives and for referendums or plebiscites. Voting in an election gives citizens a chance to decide who will represent them in government. Voting in a referendum allows citizens to personally choose how they would like to see a local or provincial issue decided (direct democracy). Many citizens become even more involved in the decision-making process by taking part as a candidate in an election themselves. Whether running as a candidate in a local council or at the provincial or federal level, becoming an elected representative allows citizens the opportunity to take part in government to an even greater extent.

One way that citizens have tried in the past to actively influence political decisions is to form a lobby group. Lobbying can involve contributing time or certain skills to a political party.

Citizens can also participate in government decision-making by attending public meetings. At the meeting, individuals or groups can voice their opinions or express their dislike for potential laws or actions proposed by the government. Citizens or groups of citizens can also identify a need or concern in their community or at the provincial level and work together for a possible solution. They may choose to conduct a petition where people can sign their names to support a change they feel should be made.

Associations can also be influential in expressing their concerns to government representatives. These concerns can be taken to a particular committee or department to be addressed and discussed. Some groups form **grassroots organizations** to study issues and follow government actions to ensure that the government is accountable to citizens. With such a large membership, they can be more effective than individuals alone. There are also large, sometimes international **non-governmental organizations** that form. They have many volunteers and often community support and donations to help them monitor government actions. The input of these groups can be very influential to government. An example of a non-governmental group is the Sierra Club Canada, which monitors our natural environment.

Groups and associations may gather information that can assist government in making decisions. For example, a concern for the safety of motorists on Alberta highways and wildlife conservation has existed for many years. This issue is of particular concern where highways span densely forested areas because large numbers of wildlife tend to live in these natural habitats. In response to this concern, the Miistakis Institute, which is located at the University of Calgary, initiated a Road Watch program. In this program, data about the movement of wildlife, such as deer and elk, in the Crowsnest Pass area is tracked and recorded by local volunteers. This information is then passed to the Department of Transportation in our province. The department can decide what highway improvements need to be made, where to build wildlife crossing passes, and whether to build underpasses or fenced overpasses. The efforts of the Miistakis Institute and volunteers who contribute to the Road Watch program have helped to provide an ongoing solution to this very important issue. This is an example of the valuable contributions that groups of Albertans and individual citizens have made toward influencing the decision-making process in our province.

There are also many ways that students can participate in the decision-making process. One way is by taking part in school government as a student representative. Many schools have an elected student leadership council that works on issues and interests in their schools and takes part in charitable causes. Students can choose to participate as a candidate for a student leadership position or vote for their choice of student representative. Students can also find out about issues or individuals in their community, province, or worldwide that require help. They can research the issue and bring it to the awareness of a local council member.

Equality and fairness should exist for all members of our communities. Citizens and groups have a responsibility to express any concern they have with unfairness or inequalities in our society. If you wonder about a particular situation or community issue, you can read through our Canadian Charter of Rights and Freedoms. The rights and freedoms of all Canadian citizens are contained in it.

Many individuals, associations, and groups within Alberta volunteer their time to participate in the decision-making process regarding issues in their communities or in the province. Their efforts are invaluable in assisting and influencing our government to work toward changes that help shape our communities and assist with concerns in other parts of the world as well. The process of participation makes our democratic system of government stronger.

Practice Questions: 26, 27

6.1.6.2 How do associations such as the Association canadienne-francaise de l'Alberta (ACFA), the Metis Nation of Alberta Association (MNAA), and the First Nations Authorities (FNA) provide their members with a voice at local and provincial levels to exercise historical and constitutional rights?

ASSOCIATIONS AND HISTORICAL AND CONSTITUTIONAL RIGHTS

The Association canadienne-francaise de l'Alberta (ACFA), the Metis Nation of Alberta Association (MNAA), and the First Nations Authorities (FNA) all actively promote the needs and concerns of their members. These associations seek to preserve and protect the historical, collective, and constitutional rights of each of these groups.

THE ASSOCIATION CANADIENNE-FRANÇAISE DE L'ALBERTA (ACFA)

Alberta was created as a province in 1905 when the federal government passed the Alberta Act. French was a recognized language in the province at that time, and the Alberta Act was written in both English and French. Because of the fur trade, French was the first European language that was spoken in Alberta. As well, a sizable francophone population existed in many Alberta communities during the late 1800s. A strong French community also existed in Edmonton. At the turn of the century, many French and English businesses existed in Edmonton. There was a French newspaper and an English newspaper. One of Edmonton's three banks was French-Canadian, and French professionals held many high positions in the community.

Although there was a strong French presence in the new capital of Edmonton, Alberta's French-speaking population was a minority of about 15%. Minority language rights were not mentioned in the Alberta Act. A wave of immigration during the following decades did not bring large numbers of French-Canadians to Alberta as the religious leaders in the province had hoped.

In 1892, legislation concerning schools stated that instruction was to be provided in English only. A later modification to this ruling in 1901 allowed French to be taught as a primary course when the population warranted it. Because of the dwindling numbers of French immigrants moving to Alberta, the francophone population had to struggle to maintain its culture in the province over the coming years.

In response, The Association canadienne-francaise de l'Alberta (ACFA) was formed in 1926 to act on behalf of francophone Albertans. It worked to protect their interests and preserve their culture and identity in the province. The ACFA has actively taken part in addressing a number of issues concerning francophone rights since that time. Historically, the ACFA has worked on many projects and agreements that have established francophone rights, both historic and constitutional. One area of prime concern is the delivery of francophone education in the province. The ACFA has worked closely with francophone parents over the years to protect francophone interests in education.

Several of the activities the ACFA has taken on in our province to protect and promote the francophone culture and rights are listed here.

- 1928—It started the newspaper *La Survivance*, which was renamed the *Franco-Albertain* in 1967.

- 1946—It established French library services, and later established bookstore services as well.

- 1949—It started a French language radio broadcast.

- 1960—It created five regional groups to oversee ACFA activities and respond to francophone needs.

- 1968—It was involved in the Alberta School Act being amended to allow 50% French instruction daily, which was increased to 80% a few years later.

- 1970—It started French television broadcasting.

- 1977—It established the Bureau de l'éducation that actively plays a role in developing French immersion programs in Alberta.

- 1982—According to Section 23 of the Canadian Charter of Rights and Freedoms, the education rights of anglophone and francophone minorities across Canada were recognized. The ACFA played a large role in actively working with the courts, parents, school board authorities, and government officials in addressing francophone minority language rights in education. The ACFA conducted two large studies about francophone schooling that (1) presented francophone community expectations toward francophone schooling, and (2) helped the francophone community present a unified voice in negotiating with the Alberta government in the management of francophone schools.

- 1993—The ACFA worked for more that a decade following the Charter with francophone parents to realize francophone minority language rights for their children in education. During this time, court cases challenging official language minority rights took place in Alberta and finally in the Supreme Court of Canada. The Supreme Court recognized that francophone parents did have a right to participate in and manage their children's education in francophone communities with large enough populations. Thus, the Alberta government did grant francophone citizens the right to francophone education and the creation of francophone school boards.

- 1999—It helped create five francophone school boards in the province.

- 1999—It created the Secrétariat francophone to represent the needs of the Franco-Albertan community within government, work toward ensuring francophone rights, and promote the French culture and language in Alberta.

- Today, the ACFA works closely with Francophone citizens, nearly 200 regional and provincial organizations, and the Alberta government. There are now approximately 65 000 French-speaking citizens throughout the province. The ACFA continues to be their representative voice and works toward building strong and vibrant francophone communities.

PARTS OF THE CONSTITUTION ACT THAT REFER TO THE RIGHTS & FREEDOMS OF CANADA'S ABORIGINAL PEOPLES

PART I (Sections 1 to 34) of the CONSTITUTION ACT, 1982 is the CANADIAN CHARTER OF RIGHTS AND FREEDOMS

Section 25: refers to the freedoms and rights of aboriginal peoples in Canada. This section states that the guarantee of certain freedoms and rights written in the Charter does not affect or take away from any previous "aboriginal, treaty or other rights or freedoms that pertain to the aboriginal peoples of Canada including any rights or freedoms that have been recognized by the Royal Proclamation of October 7, 1763; and any rights or freedoms that now exist by way of land claims agreements or may be so acquired."

Part II (Sections 35 and 35.1) of the CONSTITUTION ACT, 1982 is the RIGHTS OF THE ABORIGINAL PEOPLES OF CANADA

Section 35:

(1) Recognizes and affirms "existing aboriginal and treaty rights"

(2) Defines that " 'aboriginal peoples of Canada' includes the Indian, Inuit and Métis peoples of Canada"

(3) Clarifies that " 'treaty rights' includes rights that now exist by way of land claims agreements or may be so acquired."

(4) Guarantees "aboriginal and treaty rights...equally to male and female persons."

Section 35.1 (this section was added by amendment in 1983):

This section explains that before any amendment (altering) can ever be made to those sections of the Constitution Act that specifically address Canada's Aboriginal peoples (Section 91, Class 24 of the **Constitution Act, 1867 (BNA Act)** or **Sections 25 or 35 of the Constitution Act, 1982**), then,

(*a*) a constitutional conference with an agenda that includes the proposed amendment will be arranged by the Prime Minister and attended by the Prime Minister and the provincial leaders,

and,

(*b*) the Prime Minister "will invite representatives of the aboriginal peoples of Canada to participate in the discussions on that item."

FIRST NATIONS AUTHORITIES (FNA)

Both the Treaty of La Grande Paix de Montréal (1701) and the Royal Proclamation (1763) respected the rights of Canada's Aboriginal Peoples in a democratic manner.
Aboriginal Peoples were viewed as independent groups who had the right to their own territories and self-government. However, when the country of Canada was created through Confederation in 1867, Canada's Aboriginal Peoples lost the ability to self-govern. The British North America Act (BNA), also referred to as the Constitution Act, was passed in 1867. One section of the Act gave the federal government legislative authority over Canada's Aboriginal Peoples and the lands that were reserved for them. Canada's Aboriginal Peoples had not been asked to take part in the making of the BNA; furthermore, they did not sign it. Over time, Canada's Aboriginal Peoples have sought to regain the rights that they once had. It was in 1960 that First Nations could vote for the first time in federal elections without having to give up their First Nations status, which meant giving up particular First Nations rights.

During the late 1800s and early 1900s, a number of treaties were signed between First Nations and the Canadian government. These treaties involved an exchange of First Nations lands for particular rights and payments from the federal government. The treaty rights included special land rights and entitlements. Some agreements during the treaty negotiations were spoken and therefore, were not written in the treaty documents. First Nations viewed the treaties as a partnership between themselves and the Government of Canada.

To this day, First Nations consider the treaties to be sacred as well as legal documents. These treaties remain a key factor in the relationship between the Alberta government and First Nations peoples, leaders, and organizations. Canadian courts interpret treaty claims to see that they respect treaty rights. Section 35 of the Constitution Act (1982) recognizes and affirms "existing aboriginal and treaty rights" and states that the treaty rights include "rights that now exist by way of land claims agreements or may be so acquired." Additionally, during Treaty Table talks, the Alberta government and First Nations representatives discuss the Treaties.

First Nations Authorities in Alberta

First Nations Chiefs and Councils are the governing authorities that act on behalf of Alberta's 46 First Nations at the local level of government. The First Nations communities in Alberta include the Stoney, Tsu'u T'ina, Woodland Cree, Plains Cree, Beaver Lake, Chipewyan, and Slavey communities. All of the First Nations belong to one of the three treaty organizations in the province. These treaty organizations are (a) the Confederacy of Treaty 6 First Nations, (b) Treaty 7 First Nations, or (c) Treaty 8 First Nations of Alberta. Treaty 8, which occurred in 1899, was the last treaty agreement that took place between the First Nations and the Government of Canada in what is now Alberta.

First Nations Councils of today grew from the councils that were created during the latter part of the 1900s. They have an elected type of government and oversee local matters affecting their communities. As First Nations Authorities, the First Nations Chiefs and Councils have gained more power over time to manage their communities and control some matters that directly affect First Nations peoples.

Other First Nations Authorities

The First Nations Educational Authority, provided for in 1973 by the Government of Canada, granted First Nations in Alberta the ability to control their own local education. As a result, a number of First Nations Education Authorities and school boards have been established in Alberta. More than 50 First Nations schools exist throughout the province. An example of a First Nations Education Authority is the Little Red River Board of Education. The Board oversees the educational needs of the Little Red River Cree Nation, which is located in northern Alberta. In 1984, the Little Red River Cree Nation Chief and Council decided to run their own system of education. There are three communities in this First Nation with a combined population of approximately 4 300 people. Education is an important part of the communities. There are three schools, one in each community, and the Woodlands Cree language is spoken in all three.

The First Nations Finance Authority, established in 1995, is a non-profit authority that was created to serve First Nations governments. The Authority issues bonds on behalf of the First Nations governments, and the proceeds are used to build infrastructure, such as water treatment facilities, roads, and sewer systems in First Nations communities.

The First Nations Police Governance Authority, established in 2002, is another example of a First Nations authority. This authority is in charge of overseeing police training for the more than 40 self-administered First Nations Police Services in communities throughout Canada.

The Alberta Treaty 8 Health Authority provides for the health needs of the Alberta Treaty 8 Nation communities. The Treaty 8 Nation communities are located in the northern part of the province. The Authority is actively involved in taking care of the health and well-being of its First Nations people.

The Métis Nation of Alberta Association (MNAA)

The Métis people are people whose ancestry is that of First Nations and European cultures. The ancestral origins for the Métis people include the Ojibway, Cree, Irish, French, and Scottish cultures.

The Royal Proclamation of 1763 stated the relationship that would exist between the Aboriginal Peoples and the British government in what is today known as Canada. In the Royal Proclamation, the First Nations were referred to as independent groups who had the right to their own territories and their own government. Their lands were not to be taken from them without their agreement. The federal government did not follow the Proclamation with regard to the Métis people. As a result, the Métis felt that this treatment was unjust and did not respect their historic rights.

The Métis Nation of Alberta Association (MNAA) was formed in 1932 to act on behalf of Alberta's Métis. The MNAA promotes the cultural, economic, educational, political, and social development of Métis people in Alberta.

The Constitution Act in 1982 officially established Métis rights in Alberta and in Canada. One section of the act defined Canada's Aboriginal Peoples to include "the Indian, Inuit and Métis peoples of Canada." Because of this, the Métis were now officially recognized in Canada's Constitution. Another section recognized the existing aboriginal and treaty rights for Canada's Aboriginal Peoples. These rights now belong to Canada's Métis as well.

The MNAA works toward gaining historic and constitutional rights for the Métis. The rights that they seek involve two different categories: "land and resource rights and self-governing rights." One concern which the MNAA addressed to the Alberta government was the need to create distinct Métis settlements. The government created twelve Métis settlements that were later reduced to eight. Local councils govern the settlements whose councillors combine to form the 40 member **Métis Settlements General Council**. All other Métis in the province are governed by the Provincial Council of Métis Nation of Alberta.

Rights for land and resources have also been sought by the Métis in their traditionally settled lands. This also includes rights to resources above and below the ground, hunting animals for food, and extracting minerals.

The MNAA has been very involved over time with the issue of **harvesting rights**, which refers to the Métis ability to gather renewable resources such as wildlife and plants for food. Use of the land is part of the the Métis traditional way of life that respects nature and the conservation of resources. This, in turn, promotes a sustainable natural environment for generations to come. The Métis view harvesting rights as part of their collective rights as an aboriginal group of people in Canada.

The MNAA continues to work for the Métis people to promote their culture and establish their historical and constitutional rights.

Practice Questions: 28, 29

6.1.6.3 In what ways do elected officials demonstrate their accountability to the electorate?

ELECTED OFFICIALS AND ACCOUNTABILITY TO THE ELECTORATE

It is the responsibility of elected officials to be accountable to all of the citizens (constituents) living in the constituency where they are elected. This even includes constituents who did not vote for the elected official. Elected officials are responsible for serving citizen's political needs and representing and expressing their concerns in government meetings. They must also consider the common good of all citizens in their decision-making. At the executive level, the Premier and the cabinet have a responsibility to make decisions, provide services, and take actions that are in the best interest of all of Alberta's citizens, not just those citizens living in their own constituencies.

Because municipal councillors and provincial MLAs have been elected to serve their wards and constituencies, they are expected to listen carefully to citizens' concerns. Where appropriate, they should take citizen's concerns to the particular government departments where they can be addressed. This accountability is necessary for representative government to work for citizens and to ensure that their voices are always heard. Often, citizens in a ward or a constituency have differing points of view about issues. Representatives do their best to hear what everyone has to say before making a decision or voting on a bylaw (local level) or bill (provincial level). They try to consider the needs of all citizens fairly.

Elected officials demonstrate their accountability to the electorate in a number of ways. These ways focus on effective two-way communication, addressing needs, and strengthening and building communities. Elected officials try to be actively involved in their community and often attend government-sponsored local events and functions. MLAs usually maintain a constituency office where citizens can meet to discuss matters. Elected officials are expected to talk with constituents, listen to their concerns, and seek solutions. As well as listening to the concerns of constituents, elected officials are also responsible for keeping constituents informed about government policies, programs, and spending through newsletters, various media sources, and other forms of communication.

The cornerstone of representative government is that elected officials are accountable to the citizens they represent. In a democratic system, elected officials must represent the viewpoints and concerns of citizens living in their constituencies. However, they must also be responsible to act in the best interests of those constituents as well. No elected officials are ever above the law, and they must obey the law as well. This principle is known as **rule of law**. In other words, they must make their decisions based on what their constituents want and what is best for Alberta's citizens. What they personally think about a particular issue is not important. Elected officials should refer to the Charter and ensure that the rights and freedoms of the citizens they represent are always respected and protected.

Following the democratic principles of justice, equity, freedoms, and representation while doing their work enables elected officials to continually demonstrate their accountability to the electorate. As a result, an effective and dynamic working relationship can develop between citizens and government. This relationship can strengthen our democracy, effectively serve the needs of citizens, protect our rights and freedoms, and shape strong and sustainable communities.

Practice Question: 30

PRACTICE QUESTIONS—CITIZENS PARTICIPATING IN DECISION-MAKING

Use the following information to answer the next question.

During elections, citizens can vote for a candidate who expresses their concerns and viewpoints to government.

1. Which of the following principles of democracy is **most likely** associated with the given statement?

   A. Equity

   B. Justice

   C. Freedoms

   D. Representation

Use the following information to answer the next question.

During the early 1200s, nobles in England took part in uprisings against King John. The nobles were unhappy that the King unfairly taxed them, wrongly imprisoned and punished them, and passed laws without consulting the people. The King did not have to follow the law. Under pressure from the growing discontent, the King signed a charter called the Magna Carta in 1215. The Magna Carta limited the power that the King had over the people and ensured that everyone, including the King, had to obey the law. In return, the nobles promised to support the King. Historically, the Magna Carta was a major step toward democracy.

2. The **main** intent of the nobles in creating the Magna Carta was **most likely** to ensure

   A. equal rights among all persons

   B. representative government

   C. responsible government

   D. low taxes for the nobles

3. A plebiscite is a procedure that can be described **best** as which of the following forms of democracy?

   A. Representative government

   B. Constitutional government

   C. Majority government

   D. Direct government

Use the following information to answer the next question.

> All Canadian citizens have the right to vote, and citizens have the responsibility to be informed. In order to be informed, citizens need to learn about candidates and about issues prior to an election.

4. The **most** effective way to learn about issues prior to an election is to

   A. study newspapers and news magazines

   B. discuss issues with friends and acquaintances

   C. research issues using *The Canadian Encyclopedia*

   D. watch the television news or listen to the radio news

Use the following information to answer the next question.

> Canada's justice system seeks to protect the democratic and constitutional rights of Canadians by ensuring that laws are obeyed, and that the rights and freedoms contained in the Canadian Charter of Rights and Freedoms are respected.

5. Laws that are interpreted by Canada's justice system were originally the result of

   A. votes cast by Canadian citizens

   B. agreements made between individuals

   C. legislative decisions made by politicians

   D. agreements made between groups of individuals and organizations

Use the following information to answer the next question.

> Canadian citizens with permanent residency have the right to move to a different province and choose a different type of work.

6. The given statement **most likely** refers to which of the following types of rights from the Canadian Charter of Rights and Freedoms?

   A. Legal rights

   B. Mobility rights

   C. Equality rights

   D. Democratic rights

7. The **main** reason that both the French and English languages are used in the federal government's services and communications is that

   A. Canada has two official languages

   B. most citizens in Canada are bilingual

   C. both French and English are used to teach students in Canadian schools

   D. more services can be provided to citizens by offering them in two languages

Use the following information to answer the next question.

> The Canadian Charter of Rights and Freedoms protects the collective rights of official language minorities in Canada.

8. Which of the following groups of people would **most likely** be considered an official language minority in Canada?

   A. French-speaking Canadians living in Montreal

   B. Italian-speaking Canadians living in Lethbridge

   C. English-speaking Canadians living in Quebec City

   D. German-speaking Canadians living in Grande Prairie

9. All of the following rights are considered collective and constitutional rights that Aboriginal peoples in Canada have or may seek in the future **except**

   A. the right to separate from Canada

   B. the right to particular lands

   C. the right to mineral profits

   D. the right to self-govern

10. Considering the long-term effects, which of the following statements best explains the outcome of the signing of the Treaty of La Grande Paix de Montréal?

    A. The Treaty was a success because the feelings of compromise and respect for collective rights that developed between each First Nations group and the French during Treaty negotiations continued on for years to come.

    B. The Treaty was a success because the colony of Montréal grew and prospered when the First Nations groups who were allies and enemies of the French ended their own conflicts.

    C. The Treaty was a failure because several First Nations groups and the French did not respect each other's collective rights when using the hunting lands near Lake Ontario.

    D. The Treaty was a failure because the main goal of the Governor of New France was to protect the fur trade, but the Treaty gave control of the fur trade to the First Nations.

11. In comparing the Treaty of La Grande Paix de Montréal (1701) to the Canadian Charter of Rights and Freedoms (1982), which of the following conclusions can **most likely** be made?

    A. Only the Charter respected the collective identity of First Nations groups.

    B. Both the Treaty and the Charter can be considered human rights documents.

    C. Neither the Treaty nor the Charter addressed the issue of equality among cultures.

    D. Rights within the Charter give Canada's Aboriginal peoples more independence today than they had at the time of the Treaty.

12. As it is used in the phrase "the Canadian Charter of Rights and Freedoms is entrenched in the Constitution of Canada," the **best** meaning of the word "entrenched" is

A. attached

B. cemented

C. pasted firmly

D. written securely

Use the following information to answer the next question.

Mrs. Martens has been closely following the campaigns of candidates running in her city's upcoming local election. She has been particularly impressed by the viewpoints of Candidate Leong, who seeks to represent the ward in which Mrs. Martens lives. But Mrs. Martens feels that she would like more information in order to make her final decision about which candidate to vote for.

13. Which of the following activities would likely help Mrs. Martens the **most** in making her decision about the candidate to vote for?

A. Watching a news special about all the candidates

B. Attending rallies being held by all of the candidates

C. Phoning Candidate Leong and asking her some questions

D. Reading Candidate Leong's biography about her previous experience

14. Many local officials are elected to their positions; some are hired. All of the following positions are elected **except** that of a

A. city architect

B. city councillor

C. mayor

D. reeve

15. An example of a bylaw is a law that

A. forbids stealing

B. requires advertisements to be truthful

C. forces restaurants to close by 12:00 midnight

D. prohibits highway travel speeds greater than 100 km/h

Use the following information to answer the next question.

Many people in Trentville have strong opinions about a proposed recreation centre.

Speaker I

Do we really need a brand new centre? After all, we have a perfectly useable ice rink for the winter. It just needs the regular maintenance it always gets, for which we're already paying. And for the summer, we already have parks, playgrounds, and an outdoor pool. The pool does need upgrading, but we know that will only cost two million dollars.

Speaker II

The issue is perfectly clear. The responsibilities of our government are presented very clearly in law. Municipalities are responsible for parks and recreation. Our young people need healthy activity, and our town council has the obligation to do something. A new recreation centre may cost five million dollars, but the project is worth it.

Speaker III

The municipal government does have the responsibility for recreation centres. That is, if one is to be built, then a town government is responsible for building it. However, there is no law saying that a town has to have a recreation centre. Do we need a recreation centre at all? I think we are already paying enough money in taxes. In fact, we pay too much money. We should all be fit and active, but we can all look after our own health.

Speaker IV

A year-round swimming pool and year-round skating rink sure would be nice for this town. Nobody is getting enough exercise these days. But has anyone asked how much money the centre will cost every year to run? Maybe the five million dollars is just the tip of the iceberg. We might end up paying a lot more.

16. The speaker who **best** presents the viewpoint that the local government should meet its citizens' needs by building the recreation centre is

A. Speaker I

B. Speaker II

C. Speaker III

D. Speaker IV

17. The **main** reason that local urban governments often have greater numbers of elected councillors than local rural governments is that

    A. a greater number of by-elections are held in urban municipalities

    B. more people live in urban municipalities, and they need to be represented in government

    C. local urban governments have larger issues to deal with that require a greater number of councillors

    D. more government department employees work in urban municipalities, and they need councillors to supervise them

18. Which of the following statements about school boards and municipal governments is **not** true?

    A. They both have a leadership team.

    B. They both create rules to be followed.

    C. They both have budgets that must be balanced.

    D. They both have a leader that is elected by the public.

19. In which of the following areas of the Alberta government are policies **most likely** decided upon and put into practice?

    A. Constituency offices

    B. Cabinet departments

    C. The executive council

    D. The legislative assembly

20. Presently in the Alberta Legislature, which of the following government officials does **not** belong to a political party?

    A. The premier

    B. A cabinet minister

    C. The lieutenant-governor

    D. A member of the legislative assembly

21. The first reading of a bill introduced by an MLA takes place in the

    A. office of the lieutenant-governor

    B. executive council office

    C. legislative assembly

    D. cabinet

Use the following information to answer the next question.

> The Alberta new brand initiative by the Alberta government seeks to attract investment in Alberta from world markets, promote the sale of Alberta's goods and services, and draw tourists to our province.

22. The **main** intent of the Alberta government's new brand incentive is to
    A. improve Alberta's economy
    B. develop Alberta's resources
    C. promote the development of tourism in Alberta
    D. increase the Alberta government's ties to world markets

23. The **most likely** reason that Elections Canada is considering using Internet online voting during future elections in Canada is to
    A. increase candidate advertising to voters prior to elections
    B. decrease the amount of time necessary to hold elections
    C. increase the number of people voting in elections
    D. decrease the costs of holding elections

24. Different political parties in Canada **most likely** all have the same
    A. policies
    B. points of view
    C. political strategies
    D. democratic principles

25. Which of the following duties belongs to both cabinet ministers and other members of the legislative assembly (MLAs)?
    A. Working closely with the premier as part of the executive council
    B. Being responsible for a government department
    C. Representing the citizens of their constituency
    D. Overseeing particular services

Use the following information to answer the next question.

> A number of people in Trentville feel that the town needs a recreation centre. They organize themselves into a committee and research the cost of building a recreation centre. The committee talks to other people in Trentville and writes letters to *The Trentville Chronicle*, the town's newspaper. Once they have gathered information, the committee meets with the city council. The mayor and all of the councillors like the idea of a recreation centre. They know that the provincial government has put aside some money for community projects. The council thinks that the people of Trentville would approve a small tax increase to help pay for the project. However, the mayor tells the committee that at least one million dollars will have to be raised privately for the recreation centre's construction.

26. The given example **best** supports which of the following conclusions?

    A. Recreation centres are a provincial responsibility.

    B. Governments are not responsible for recreation centres.

    C. Governments and individuals cooperate to meet some needs.

    D. Community projects are mainly funded by donations from private citizens.

27. When people organize into groups to address a need that is not being met by government, they do **not** have the authority to

    A. fundraise money

    B. form committees

    C. hold elections

    D. collect taxes

Use the following information to answer the next question.

> The Métis Nation of Alberta Association (MNAA) works toward gaining historic and constitutional rights for Alberta's Métis peoples, such as the rights to land, resources, and the ability to self-govern.

28. Which of the following events **most likely** has been of greatest significance to the MNAA's work toward gaining historic and constitutional rights for the Métis peoples?

    A. The revision of the Constitution Act in 1982

    B. The creation of First Nations Authorities in Alberta

    C. The creation of the eight Métis settlements by the Alberta government

    D. The separation of the territory of Nunavut from the Northwest Territories

29. Since its formation in 1926, one of the **main** objectives achieved by the Association canadienne-francaise de l'Alberta (ACFA) over the years is **most likely** the right of Francophone children to Francophone

   A. education

   B. health care

   C. sports programs

   D. community services

30. MLAs can demonstrate their accountability to their constituents in each of the following ways **except** by

   A. holding community breakfasts for constituents

   B. representing constituents' concerns during government meetings

   C. meeting with constituents in the constituency office to hear their viewpoints

   D. making wise personal decisions in government that benefit their constituents

ANSWERS AND SOLUTIONS—PRACTICE QUESTIONS

1. D	7. A	13. B	19. C	25. C
2. C	8. C	14. A	20. C	26. C
3. D	9. A	15. C	21. C	27. D
4. A	10. A	16. B	22. A	28. A
5. C	11. B	17. B	23. C	29. A
6. B	12. D	18. D	24. D	30. D

1. D

The given statement refers to the democratic principle of representation. In Canada's representative democracy, citizens vote for a candidate to represent them and act on their behalf in government.

Equity refers to all individuals having equal opportunities. Justice refers to treating all individuals and groups fairly. Citizens of a democracy have particular freedoms, including the freedom of thought, the freedom of speech, and the freedom to vote.

2. C

In creating the Magna Carta, the nobles wanted to make the King, who was the ruler of the government, responsible to the people by having him governed by the law. The King could no longer tax or imprison people just because he wanted to. The nobles wished to be governed responsibly and fairly by the King.

The Magna Carta was a step toward ensuring that citizens' rights would be protected. However, equal rights did not exist among all persons in England at that time, and the main intent of the nobles in creating the Magna Carta was not to create equal rights for all. Nobles had a higher status than peasants and labourers, and they were most likely intent on guaranteeing their own rights.

A representative government is one in which people are elected by citizens to represent their needs in government. The intent of the nobles in creating the Magna Carta was not to have all persons presenting their needs to the king. Nor were they only concerned with unfair taxation practices. They wanted the King to be responsible in all of his actions, consult them on new laws, and not imprison them unfairly.

3. D

A referendum (plebiscite) is a form of direct government. Citizens vote directly on a proposed law. The result of their vote becomes law. In this way, people act *directly* in determining a decision made by government.

In a representative government, elected members of government act on behalf of citizens. A constitutional government is a government that is controlled by a set of laws called a constitution. A majority government occurs when over half of the candidates elected during an election belong to the same political party.

4. A

Newspapers and news magazines are most likely to have the kind of information voters need at election time. During elections, the issues often are not simple. In order to vote wisely, people need to read a lot to understand about the candidates and issues. A good newspaper will present both sides of issues and may also present an evaluation of the present government. Voters need to know if the government in power has kept its promises, and if not, why not.

Discussion with friends is very useful. However, it often occurs between people who already agree with each other or who are uninformed. *The Canadian Encyclopedia* is useful for finding out background information about Canadian issues. However, an encyclopedia cannot be completely up-to-date. Television and radio news have limited use for citizens trying to understand election issues. They both tend to have short news items that often focus on dramatic stories. Political disagreements may attract a person's attention, but understanding the issues involved takes time.

5. C

Laws are made by politicians who sit on city council, in provincial legislatures, or in Parliament. Politicians create and vote on laws to be passed.

Canadian citizens vote for representatives who sit on city council, in provincial legislatures, or in Parliament. As part of their political duties, these politicians create and vote on laws to be passed. Agreements between individuals or between groups of individuals and organizations are called contracts. Contracts are only for the people involved. Laws apply to everyone.

6. B

Mobility rights allow Canadian citizens with permanent residency to live, work, or travel anywhere in Canada.

Legal rights refer to those rights that protect the safety of Canadian citizens and that deal with situations of legal conflict. Equality rights are those rights that ensure fair and equal treatment to all Canadian citizens. Democratic rights refer to the right of all Canadian citizens to vote for representatives who will express their viewpoints in government.

7. A

French and English are officially used in Parliamentary and government institutions, communications, and services because Canada has two official languages. Official language rights concerning English and French are referred to in the Canadian Charter of Rights and Freedoms. Canada has a long history of two official languages, and government institutions must provide communications and services to customers in the official language of their choice.

Many citizens in Canada are bilingual in both French and English. However, many other Canadians are bilingual in a combination of either English and one of many other languages, or French and one of many other languages. Some Canadians speak multiple languages, but the majority of Canadians do speak French, or English, or both.

Although both French and English are commonly used for educational instruction in Canada, this is not the main reason for their use in federal government communications and services. Nor is providing more services the main reason for their use by the federal government.

8. **C**

English-speaking Canadians living in Quebec City would be considered an official language minority in Canada as the majority of people living in Quebec City speak French.

French-speaking Canadians living in Montreal would not be considered an official language minority as the majority of people living in Montreal speak French. Neither Italian nor German is one of Canada's two official languages. English and French are Canada's two official languages.

9. **A**

The right to separate from Canada is not a collective or constitutional right. There is no reference to sovereignty, or the right to separate from Canada, in the Constitution Act (1982).

The right to particular lands established in treaties is a collective and constitutional right. Many Aboriginal land claims have been resolved, or are being considered, since the Constitution Act was revised in 1982 and included the newly created Canadian Charter of Rights and Freedoms. The right to mineral resources above and below the ground in particular lands belonging to Canada's Aboriginal peoples is a collective and constitutional right. Land claims often involve establishing the rights to minerals or resources. Canada's Aboriginal peoples seek self-government, and local forms of self-government do exist. The Royal Proclamation (1763) viewed Aboriginal peoples as independent groups with the right to their own territories and self-government within the territories controlled by Britain. The Canadian Charter of Rights and Freedoms supports and does not change the rights guaranteed to Canada's Aboriginal peoples in the Royal Proclamation.

10. **A**

The Treaty was a success. The main terms of the Treaty of La Grande Paix emerged through the use of cooperation, diplomacy, and respect for the common good and collective rights of all attending First Nations groups and the French. The Treaty was a success because the goodwill and respect expressed by each group during Treaty negotiations continued on in years to come. As a result, unhampered by warfare, the colony of Montréal grew, and the French fur trade prospered.

The Treaty was not a failure. The First Nations groups respected the collective rights of each other in the use of hunting lands adjacent to Lake Ontario. The French kept control of the fur trade, and the conflict between warring groups ended. The colony of Montréal grew and prospered because of the feelings of compromise and respect that had emerged during the Treaty negotiations. This respect and diplomacy prevented warfare from occurring that would have negatively affected the colony of Montréal and the fur trade.

11. B

Both the Treaty and the Charter can be considered human rights documents. The Treaty negotiations were carried out with the highest respect for all groups involved. All representatives spoke their points of view and were listened to intently. Collective and individual rights were respected. The Charter can also be considered a human rights document. Even its name, the Canadian Charter of Rights and Freedoms, refers to the fact that its contents define human rights and freedoms in Canada.

Both the Treaty of La Grande Paix and the Canadian Charter of Rights and Freedoms recognize equality among cultures. Both the Treaty and the Charter respect the collective identity of Canada's Aboriginal peoples. Collective and constitutional rights within the Charter do not give Canada's Aboriginal peoples more independence today than they had at the time of the Treaty in 1701. The Treaty recognized the First Nations as completely independent nations with their own territories, self-government, and hunting rights. The Charter recognizes all previous constitutional and collective rights of Canada's Aboriginal peoples.

12. D

The Charter is written securely into the Constitution Act, 1982 as Part I (Sections 1 to 34).

The Constitution of Canada is an official document, which is called the Constitution Act, 1982. The Charter is a securely written part of the Constitution Act. It is not cemented, attached, or pasted to the front, back, or inside of the Constitution Act.

13. B

Attending rallies in person gives a constituent a first-hand look at candidates expressing their points of view on different issues. In order to make a final decision about whether to vote for Candidate Leong, Mrs. Martens should seek information about all of the candidates. Then, she can compare their positions and make her decision with the greatest amount of information.

Bias sometimes occurs in media presentations, and a news special may not be long enough for a detailed look at all candidates. Asking Candidate Leong questions could be helpful, but any candidate's time for conversation would be very limited during campaigning. Mrs. Martens might be able to ask Candidate Leong and other candidates questions at a rally and could receive a greater amount of information with which to compare views. Reading over a candidate's biography would give information about past experience, but may not give up-to-date information about views on local election issues.

14. A

A city architect is a professional person who is hired by a local government. He or she designs government buildings or facilities. Local governments also employ many other workers to provide services to the public.

Government representatives, including councillors and the mayor, are elected to their positions. Mayors are leaders of local governments in urban settings. Reeves are leaders of local governments in rural settings.

15. C

Bylaws about restaurant hours are made by local governments to suit local conditions. Bylaws are local forms of law that have less serious penalties if they are broken.

Stealing is a criminal law. The federal government makes criminal laws.

Truthful statements in advertising are not a municipal government responsibility. The federal government passes laws regarding truth in advertising. Highway travel speeds are not determined by local government bylaws.

16. B

Speaker II is of the opinion that the local government has the responsibility and obligation to build a recreation centre in order to meet the needs of young people in the community.

Speakers I and IV do not mention the government's responsibility in meeting citizens' needs. Speaker III does mention the government's responsibility for building recreation centres, but does not believe that one should be built in Trentville.

17. B

Greater numbers of people live in urban municipalities; therefore, a greater number of councillors is required to represent all the constituents.

By-elections are held when councillors' positions become vacant. For example, if a councillor retires during their term in office, a by-election is held to fill that position. Having a greater number of by-elections would not be a reason to have more councillors serving on local government. Local urban governments may have more or larger issues to deal with, but this would not necessitate the election of more councillors. Councillors are elected based upon the population base of a municipality. Councillors are not required to supervise government department employees.

18. D

Municipal governments have an elected mayor, but school boards have a hired superintendent, as well as elected trustees.

School boards and municipal governments both have a leadership team that governs and has authority. School boards are called local authorities and are governed by a superintendent and trustees. Municipal governments are governed by a mayor and councillors. School boards and municipal governments both create rules that are to be followed. School boards create rules that must be followed in schools. Municipal governments create bylaws. Both school boards and municipal governments have a budget that they must balance and manage.

19. C

The executive council puts government policies into action.

Government policies are not decided upon and put into practice in MLAs' constituency offices or cabinet departments. Nor are they decided upon and put into practice in the legislative assembly, where laws are created.

20. C

The lieutenant-governor does not belong to any political party and does not favour the political party in power, nor any other political party.

The premier is the leader of the political party that has the most MLAs elected during an election. Cabinet ministers are MLAs from the political party in power who have been appointed by the premier to their cabinet position. MLAs in provincial elections predominantly are members of a particular political party, although a candidate can run as an independent and be elected.

21. C

A bill (proposed law) is introduced by an MLA, and a first reading takes place in the legislative assembly. Following study and public input, the bill has a second reading in the legislative assembly. After debate, a vote is taken regarding the bill. If supported, the bill has a third reading, followed by another vote in the legislative assembly. If, again, the bill receives a majority of support from the MLAs, it is signed by the lieutenant-governor, upon which the bill becomes law.

The office of the lieutenant-governor does not introduce bills. However, if a bill receives a majority of the MLAs' approval during a vote following its third reading, it is signed by the lieutenant-governor and becomes law. Bills are not introduced in the executive council office. The executive council consists of the premier and his or her cabinet. Bills are not introduced by cabinet ministers in the cabinet.

22. A

The main intent of the Alberta new brand initiative is most likely to improve Alberta's economy so that the province has economic sustainability for present and future generations.

In the face of the recent global recession, Alberta's new brand incentive seeks to promote our province's resources, attract investment in the province from markets around the world, and increase tourism in Alberta; however, these are all done with the goal of improving and strengthening the economy.

23. C

Elections Canada is considering the idea of online voting in order to provide convenience in voting, thus increasing the number of eligible Canadian citizens who would vote in elections.

Increasing candidate advertising to voters is not the main reason that Elections Canada is considering online voting. The amount of time required to hold elections may not increase or decrease if online voting comes into use. Decreasing the costs of holding elections is not the main reason that Elections Canada is considering online voting.

24. D

Since Canada has a democratic system of government, different political parties most likely support very similar democratic principles of equality, fairness, representation, and fundamental freedoms.

Different political parties have differing ideas, however. During elections, political parties stress their differences in policies, points of view, and strategies in order to set themselves apart from each other. They want to show why they are the better political party to vote for.

25. C

MLAs who are appointed by the premier to his cabinet are called cabinet ministers. Cabinet ministers are elected MLAs for their constituencies and, just like other MLAs, represent the citizens of their constituency in government matters.

Cabinet ministers and the premier form the executive council. Cabinet ministers work closely with the premier in the executive council, making decisions, developing strategies, and taking action on issues. Cabinet ministers are responsible for a particular government department and for overseeing the particular services of that department. MLAs who are not cabinet ministers are not responsible for a government department or particular government services.

26. C

Governments and individuals do cooperate to meet some needs. Sometimes a government will use tax money to fund part of a project. Individuals or private organizations then supply the rest of the money. In the given example, the government and citizens both like the idea of the recreation centre. Some funding for the centre could come from both provincial and municipal governments. However, the mayor indicates that private funding will be necessary for the project, as well.

The example does not make a direct statement about government responsibility for the recreation centre. However, the committee does approach their local government, not their provincial government. The text also indicates that governments have some responsibility for recreation centres. The mayor tells the committee that at least one million dollars will have to be raised privately for the project. However, the text does not indicate that this is the majority of the funding required.

27. D

Only governments can collect taxes. Private citizens do not have the authority to collect taxes.

Private groups raise most of their money for projects and activities by fundraising. Any group of people can form a committee to support an issue or get a task done. Groups of people can hold elections amongst themselves. Clubs often hold elections to choose leaders and fill positions of responsibility.

28. A

The revision of the Constitution Act of 1982 was an extremely important event for the Métis. For the first time in constitutional history, Section 35 of the Constitution Act of 1982 recognized the Métis as one of Canada's Aboriginal peoples. Also, Part I of the Constitution Act of 1982 is the Canadian Charter of Rights and Freedoms, which recognizes the provisions of previous treaties and those of the Royal Proclamation (1763). The Royal Proclamation stated that Canada's Aboriginal peoples should have the right to their own territories and self-government, those territories being considered under Britain's control. Thus, the Constitution Act, including the Charter, opened up possibilities for dialogue about historical and constitutional rights for the Métis peoples.

First Nations Authorities are a form of local government that serves Alberta's First Nations peoples. The Métis have their own form of local government and, thus, this event would not have been of the greatest significance to the MNAA. The creation of 12 Métis settlements was very important, but in terms of future discussions concerning constitutional and historic rights, the revision of the Constitution Act probably had the greatest long-term impact. Eligible voters in the Northwest Territories decided by plebiscite to divide the Northwest Territories and, as a result, the territory of Nunavut was created. This event would not have been of the greatest significance to the MNAA.

29. A

The ACFA has taken an active part over the years in representing the need of Francophone parents to have Francophone education for their children. Additionally, since the Charter was created in 1982, the ACFA has worked with the courts, parents, school board authorities, and the government to make sure that Francophone language minority rights are protected and that Francophone school boards can be formed to oversee Francophone education.

Although health care, sports programs, and community services are important to many Albertans, one of the main objectives of the ACFA has been to ensure that Francophone children have the opportunity to have a Francophone education.

30. D

MLAs should make decisions based upon the needs and viewpoints of their constituents and not upon their own personal opinions. MLAs are supposed to represent their constituents in government.

MLAs do host community breakfasts (e.g., at shopping plazas) and other local events in their respective constituencies. These are opportunities to communicate in person with their constituents. MLAs also maintain constituency offices in which they can meet with their constituents to hear their viewpoints or concerns. MLAs have a responsibility to represent their constituents' concerns during government meetings.

UNIT TEST—CITIZENS PARTICIPATING IN DECISION-MAKING

Use the following information to answer the next question.

1. Which of the following statements **best** represents the artist's message in the given drawing?

   A. Government offers many career opportunities when a person is older.

   B. Government acts as a window from which to view the world.

   C. Government is evident throughout society.

   D. Government reflects society's values.

Use the following information to answer the next question.

> During a plebiscite held in __*i*__ , a majority of the electorate voted for the creation of __*ii*__ .

2. The given statement is completed by the information in row

Row	*i*	*ii*
A.	Québec	Labrador
B.	Québec	Nunavut
C.	Northwest Territories	The Yukon Territory
D.	Northwest Territories	Nunavut

3. Which of the following examples **best** demonstrates the idea of direct democracy?

A. A teenager raising money for a local charity

B. A teenager voting on their hockey team's name

C. A teenager voting for a student government president in school

D. A teenager nominating another student to be the class representative

4. Which of the following actions is the **best** example of one responsibility of citizens in a democracy?

A. Voting wisely

B. Becoming candidates in an election

C. Writing letters to the editor of a newspaper

D. Telling friends about an important government decision

5. Following the creation of the Canadian Charter of Rights and Freedoms, Canada's justice system has needed to examine and interpret a number of appealed provincial laws in order to ensure that

A. appealed laws remain in use in Canada

B. citizens' rights and freedoms are protected

C. the collective rights of all Canadians are protected

D. provincial laws are in agreement with municipal laws

Use the following information to answer the next question.

> Girls who attended a public elementary school in a city in British Columbia during the early 1970s were not allowed to wear pants to school; only boys could wear pants. Seeing the situation as unfair, many students in the school signed a petition and, a short time later, girls were given the right to wear pants to school if they chose.

6. Which of the following rights or freedoms currently protected by the Canadian Charter of Rights and Freedoms were **most likely** in question in the given example?

   A. Fundamental freedoms

   B. Democratic rights

   C. Equality rights

   D. Mobility rights

Use the following information to answer the next question.

> During the late 1600s, continuing conflict in New France between the French, their First Nations allies, and their First Nations enemies threatened the colony of Montréal and the success of the French fur trade.

7. In order to stop the warfare and protect the colony of Montréal and the fur trade, the Governor of New France decided to give each of about 40 First Nations groups

   A. the right to vote

   B. their own independent territory

   C. an invitation to attend a large meeting

   D. representation in the government of New France

Use the following information to answer the next question.

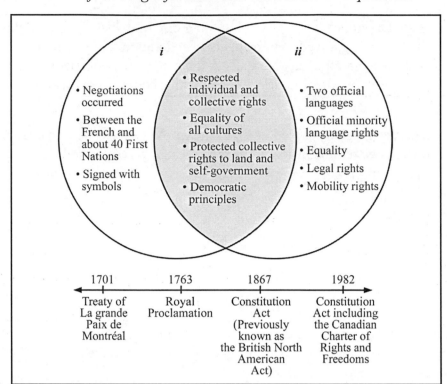

8. According to the given Venn diagram, which of the following historic events are **most likely** represented by *i* and *ii*?

	i	*ii*
A.	Royal Proclamation	British North America Act
B.	Constitution Act (1982)	Treaty of La Grande Paix
C.	Treaty of La Grande Paix	Canadian Charter of Rights and Freedoms
D.	British North America Act	Canadian Charter of Rights and Freedoms

9. The **main** reason that the Canadian Charter of Rights and Freedoms is entrenched in the Canadian Constitution is to

A. guarantee and protect the democratic rights and freedoms of Canadians

B. enable Canada's different levels of government to create new laws

C. allow collective groups in Canada to achieve self-government

D. maintain a democratic system of government in Canada

10. Which of the following criteria required for a candidate to run in a local election is incorrect?

    A. The candidate must be a Canadian citizen.

    B. The candidate must live in the municipality.

    C. The candidate must be at least 16 years of age.

    D. The candidate must be nominated by eligible voters.

Use the following information to answer the next two questions.

The town council in Trentville conducted a survey to determine if citizens felt that a new recreation centre should be built. The survey had the following results:

1. In favour of building a new recreation centre 402

2. In favour of doing nothing new 225

3. In favour of improving the existing rink, parks, playground, and swimming pool 900

4. Undecided or no opinion.. 76

11. Which of the following graphs **correctly** represents the given information?

    A.

    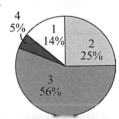

    B.

    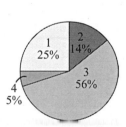

    C.

    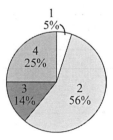

    D.

    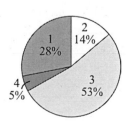

12. Based on the results of the survey, the **most likely** action that the town council in Trentville will take is to

    A. keep things as they are

    B. build a new recreation centre

    C. make improvements to existing recreation facilities

    D. conduct another survey to see if the results are the same

13. For which of the following reasons would an agricultural department be **more likely** to exist within a rural local government than an urban local government?

A. Farming occurs in rural areas.

B. The weather can be better in a rural setting than in a city.

C. People living in rural locations always require agricultural services.

D. People living in rural locations are more interested in growing their own food than people living in cities.

14. Which of the following conclusions **cannot** be made about Métis and First Nations forms of local government in Alberta?

A. Both the Métis and First Nations have representative government.

B. The Métis and the First Nations each have forms of self-government.

C. Both the Métis and First Nations have councils that make decisions for their communities.

D. The Métis and the First Nations create all of the laws that are followed in their communities.

15. Which of the following types of school boards in Alberta were **most likely** created in order to serve the needs of students with official language minority rights?

A. Public school boards

B. Charter school boards

C. Francophone school boards

D. First Nations school boards

Use the following information to answer the next question.

During the spring of 2009, the Government of Alberta announced plans to increase the number of ridings (and, therefore, also the number of MLAs) in the provincial legislature from 83 to 87.

16. The Alberta government **most likely** wants to increase the number of constituencies in Alberta in order to

A. lessen the work done by MLAs in Alberta

B. ensure that MLAs represent Alberta's growing population better

C. redraw the boundaries of constituencies in the province of Alberta

D. bring the province of Alberta in to line with requirements of the Canadian Charter of Rights and Freedoms

17. In which of the following areas of the Alberta government are laws created?

   A. Cabinet

   B. Executive council

   C. Legislative assembly

   D. Office of the lieutenant-governor

18. Which of the following statements **most likely** explains the reason for the position of lieutenant-governor in the Alberta government?

   A. Canada is a colony of Britain and, therefore, the provinces each have a lieutenant-governor.

   B. The lieutenant-governor serves as an advisor to the premier in matters of provincial and federal law.

   C. If the premier were suddenly to retire or leave office, the lieutenant-governor would become the new premier.

   D. Canada is by choice a member of the British Commonwealth, of which the lieutenant-governor is a representative.

19. The **main** responsibility for what is taught in Alberta's schools is held by

   A. the federal government

   B. municipal governments

   C. parents of schoolchildren

   D. the provincial government

20. A person **most likely** would contact the provincial government to express a concern about which of the following situations?

   A. A large number of potholes on the highway between Calgary and Edmonton

   B. An increase in the amount of property tax on a home in Red Deer

   C. An increase in vandalism in a city

   D. A lack of parks in their community

21. Which of the following persons in government would the premier **most likely** appoint to assist with decision-making and policy planning in the cabinet?

A. Any elected MLA

B. The lieutenant-governor

C. A member of the executive council

D. An elected member of the premier's political party

Use the following information to answer the next question.

A minority group of citizens would like to see a new zoo built in Brownsville. However, community support is very low, and town council members have not expressed interest in such a project.

22. Which of the following actions would be **best** for the minority group to pursue if they would like to see a new zoo built?

A. Holding a referendum on the issue

B. Holding an election vote on the issue

C. Arranging a public meeting for debate on the issue

D. Writing letters to the local newspaper expressing their point of view

Use the following information to answer the next question.

A concerned citizen writes a letter to their local newspaper. The citizen argues that municipalities have the responsibility to provide parks and recreation for their citizens. Because of that, the letter writer states that the town of Trentville has the duty to build a recreation centre and that the local government will have to find the money to meet the recreation needs of Trentville.

23. Which of the following statements is supported by the given information?

A. People should not have to raise money to build recreation centres.

B. The letter writer thinks that the town must build the recreation centre.

C. Municipal governments must meet the needs of citizens for recreation.

D. The letter writer is making a statement of fact about the duties of government.

24. Associations such as the Association canadienne-francaise de l'Alberta (ACFA), the Métis Nation of Alberta Association (MNAA), and the First Nations Authorities (FNA) **most likely** serve the interests of their members in all of the following ways **except**

    A. protecting their members' rights

    B. preserving their members' culture

    C. drafting laws to benefit their members

    D. being a voice to support their members' interests

25. Which of the following actions would be the **best** way for an elected representative to initially find out how most citizens in the community feel about an issue?

    A. Conducting a survey

    B. Talking to people individually

    C. Using advertisements to invite opinions from citizens

    D. Reading and listening to television and radio reports about the issue

1. D	6. C	11. B	16. B	21. D
2. D	7. C	12. C	17. C	22. C
3. B	8. C	13. A	18. D	23. B
4. A	9. A	14. D	19. D	24. C
5. B	10. C	15. C	20. A	25. A

1. D

The most likely intent of the drawing is to show that a democratic government is a reflection of society's values, such as fairness, rights, respect, and equity. These words, along with the government building and students, are reflected from the mirror in the drawing.

Although there are many career possibilities in government, the drawing is not intended to demonstrate that fact. The object in the drawing is meant as a mirror, not a window, so the artist's emphasis is on reflection. The idea that government is evident throughout society is general in nature, while the drawing is more likely specific in that it denotes a reflection of specific values.

2. D

A plebiscite was held in the Northwest Territories in 1992 to determine whether the majority of voters wanted the territory to be divided in two. The majority of voters did vote in favour and, as a result, Nunavut was created.

A plebiscite was not held in Quebec to determine the creation of Labrador or Nunavut.

A plebiscite was not held in the Northwest Territories to determine the creation of the Yukon.

3. B

Direct democracy is when citizens directly cast their votes to decide the outcome of a particular question. They do not have a representative make the decision on their behalf, as in representative democracy. Of the given examples, a teenager voting, along with other team members, to determine a hockey team's name demonstrates direct democracy best.

A teenager raising money for a local charity is an example of volunteerism. A teenager voting for a student government president is an example of representative democracy. The elected president would then represent and work on behalf of all students in the school. A teenager nominating another student to be the class representative is an example of representative government. If the nominated student won in the class election, he or she would then represent all the classmates.

4. A

Not only do citizens of a democracy have the right to vote in an election, they have a responsibility to vote wisely.

It is not a responsibility, or expectation, for citizens to take part as candidates in elections. However, they do have the right to take part in the political process, if they choose to. Freedom of thought is a right in Canada. It is not the responsibility of citizens, however, to share those thoughts in letters to a newspaper, unless they wish to. Freedom of speech is a right in Canada, as well. However, it is not the responsibility of citizens to share their views about government decisions with friends; they have the right to do so if they wish.

5. B

Since the Charter was written, some provincial laws have been appealed by groups or individuals to ensure that individual and collective rights and freedoms that are guaranteed in the Charter are upheld by existing laws. If, after review and interpretation of the Charter, the Supreme Court decides that the law in question is indeed in conflict with the Charter, then that provincial law becomes invalid.

An individual or group would not appeal a provincial law to ensure that the law remain in use, but instead with the hope that the law become invalid. Not all Canadians have collective rights. These rights are held by individuals that are part of a collective group, a group with a common culture, values, and historic presence in Canada. The Charter does not seek to determine if provincial laws are in agreement with municipal laws.

6. C

Equality rights, which are protected by the Charter, are those rights that ensure fair and equal treatment to all Canadian citizens. Equality rights mean that all individuals are treated equally regardless of gender, religious choice, ethnic origin, cognitive or physical impairments, or age. The given example describes girls attending a public school who did not have equality with boys in what they could wear to school.

Fundamental freedoms of Canadian citizens, which are protected by the Charter, include freedom of speech, thought, opinion, and religion. Democratic rights, which are also protected by the Charter, refer to the right of all Canadian citizens to vote for representatives who will express their viewpoints in government. Mobility rights, protected by the Charter, allow Canadian citizens with permanent residency to live, work, or travel anywhere in Canada. The given example refers to a situation involving equality rights between girls and boys.

7. C

The Governor decided to invite dozens of First Nations groups, both allies and enemies of the French, to a meeting to discuss trading and treaty partnership. The response was tremendous, and many First Nations groups attended this meeting during the summer of 1701. The meeting was a success, and the Treaty of La Grande Paix de Montréal was signed by the French and all First Nations groups attending.

The First Nations groups were not given the right to vote, their own independent territory, or representation in the government of New France.

8. C

Section *i* of the Venn diagram is representative of the Treaty of La Grande Paix. Negotiations of the Treaty were carried out in a democratic manner by the French and approximately 40 First Nations groups. All of the descriptors in Section *ii* of the Venn diagram are rights that are referred to in the Canadian Charter of Rights and Freedoms. Both of these documents were created with respect for individual and collective rights and equality of cultures, and with an acceptance of democratic principles.

Section *i* of the Venn diagram cannot represent the Royal Proclamation; the British government oversaw the Royal Proclamation, which did not consist of negotiations between the French and First Nation groups. Section *ii* of the Venn diagram cannot represent the British North America Act; when it was passed, the British North America Act did not include all of the rights in Section *ii* of the Venn diagram. Section *i* of the Venn diagram cannot represent the Constitution Act (1982) as negotiations for the Constitution Act were not carried out by the French and First Nations groups. Also, the Constitution Act was not signed with symbols.

Section *ii* of the Venn diagram cannot represent the Treaty of La Grande Paix as the Treaty did not include all of the rights in Section *ii* of the Venn diagram. Section *i* of the Venn diagram cannot represent the British North America Act because the BNA Act was overseen by the British government and did not include input from First Nations groups.

9. A

The main reason that the Canadian Charter of Rights and Freedoms is entrenched in the constitution is to guarantee and protect the democratic and constitutional rights and freedoms of Canadians. These rights and freedoms cannot be taken away by government at any point in the future because these rights are a part of the Canadian Constitution, which is the law in Canada.

Laws are created within the legislative branch of different levels of government. Thus, the Canadian Charter of Rights and Freedoms did not need to be entrenched in the Constitution to enable different levels of government to continue creating new laws. Nor is it entrenched to allow collective groups in Canada to achieve self-government. As well, Canada was maintaining a democratic system of government at the time that the Charter was created in 1982. Even if the Charter had not been entrenched in the Constitution, it is likely that the existing democratic system in Canada would have continued and been maintained. However, the Charter guarantees to protect Canadians' individual and collective rights permanently, thus permanently maintaining a democratic and free society in Canada.

10. C

A candidate must be at least 18 years of age.

A candidate must be a Canadian citizen, live in the municipality in which the election is taking place, and be nominated by eligible voters to be a candidate.

11. B

Check that each slice of the pie graph is approximately the right size and properly labelled. The total number of people surveyed is 1 603. Right away, you notice that those in favour of building a recreation centre (402 people) make up about a quarter of 1 603. Only one of the graphs has a 1/4-sized slice properly labelled "1". That is the correct graph.

12. C

The majority of respondents indicated that they would like to see improvements made to the existing rink, parks, playground, and swimming pool. Therefore, improving existing facilities is the most likely action that the town council will take.

More than 80% of respondents feel either that current recreation options need to be improved or that a new recreation centre needs to be built. Keeping things as they are is not an option for the town council. A minority of respondents would like a new recreation centre built, so there is not enough public support to build one. Since the survey clearly indicates that a minority of respondents want a new recreation centre, it is unlikely that another survey would be conducted.

13. A

Farming occurs in rural settings, not within city municipalities. Thus, a government agriculture department is more likely to offer services in a rural setting where farming takes place, rather than a city where those types of services are not required.

The weather is not necessarily better in a rural location than in a city setting. People living in rural settings do not always require agricultural services. Some local governments exist in rural communities that support primary industries other than farming, such as mining, logging, or the oil industry. Citizens living in rural settings are not necessarily more interested in growing their own food than citizens living in cities. Many citizens living in cities grow gardens from which they obtain some of their own food.

14. D

The Métis and the First Nations forms of local government can create bylaws that are followed in their communities. However, First Nations and Métis citizens, along with all Albertans, follow provincial and federal laws that are made by the provincial and federal levels of government.

Both the Métis and the First Nations have local forms of self-government that have councils representing the citizens of their communities. These councils make decisions for their communities.

15. C

Francophone school boards were created to serve the needs of Francophone communities. French is one of Canada's two official languages, English and French, but the majority of citizens in Alberta speak English as their first language. However, the Canadian Charter of Rights and Freedoms guarantees and protects official language minority rights throughout Canada. Therefore, in Alberta, Francophone parents have the right to have Francophone schools teach their children, and to have Francophone school boards run and oversee those schools in places where there are enough Francophone students. In 1999, there were five Francophone school boards created in Alberta for this purpose.

Public schools boards were not specifically created for the purpose of serving the educational needs of communities with official language minority rights. Public school boards were created to serve the needs of all children living in Alberta. Charter schools were created to provide enhanced educational programming to a specific group of students. Charter schools often have a focus on a particular area of study and are not governed by local school boards. First Nations schools provide education in First Nations languages, English, and other languages. Official language minority rights were not a factor in the creation of First Nations school boards and education authorities. In 1973, the Canadian government granted First Nations in Alberta the ability to control their own local education.

16. B

The government of Alberta wants to create four more constituencies in order to give the growing population of Alberta better representation. Alberta's population has grown by more than 1 000 000 persons since the number of constituencies was last increased, more than 20 years ago. Some constituencies (ridings) in Edmonton and Calgary have two or three times as many registered voters as areas of rural Alberta.

Increasing the number of constituencies (and the number of MLAs that represent those constituencies) from 83 to 87 likely would not lessen the workload of all MLAs, but it would mean that more MLAs spread the work around. The government of Alberta is not increasing the number of constituencies in order to redraw the electoral boundaries. Instead, the provincial government wishes to give the growing population of Alberta better representation, which requires redrawing the present constituencies. There are no requirements about number of constituencies in the Canadian Charter of Rights and Freedoms.

17. C

The legislative assembly is the area of government in which laws are created.

Laws are not created by the cabinet, the executive council, or the office of the lieutenant-governor. The executive council puts government policies into action. After a third reading, if a bill receives a majority of support from the MLAs in the legislative assembly, it is signed by the lieutenant-governor, upon which the bill becomes law.

18. D

Canada is an independent nation with control of its own Constitution. However, Canada remains, by choice, a member of the British Commonwealth, and the Queen is the head of the Commonwealth. Therefore, the governor general represents the Queen in Canada, and the lieutenant-governor of Alberta represents the Queen in the province.

Canada is an independent nation, not a colony of Britain. At one time, it was a duty of the lieutenant-governor to advise the Alberta government about the appropriateness of Alberta laws—to make sure that provincial laws were in agreement with federal laws. This is no longer the case. If the premier were suddenly to retire or leave office, the lieutenant-governor would need to ensure that the position of premier was filled. The lieutenant-governor, however, would not become the premier.

19. D

The provincial government has the main responsibility for what is taught in Alberta.

Neither the federal government nor municipal governments have the main responsibility for education in Canada. Parents have a great responsibility for their children's education. However, it is the provincial government that has the legal responsibility to organize schools and decide upon the curriculum that is taught to schoolchildren.

20. A

The provincial government is responsible for roads and highways outside of urban areas. Thus, the provincial government would hear concerns about the number of potholes on the highway between Calgary and Edmonton.

Taxes on homes are paid to the local government. Local government provides police services within cities. Community parks are also the responsibility of local government.

21. D

The premier appoints elected members (MLAs) of his or her own political party to serve in the cabinet.

MLAs are from a number of different political parties. The premiers of Alberta have historically chosen MLAs from their own political parties to serve in the cabinet.

The duties of the lieutenant-governor of Alberta do not include being a cabinet minister. Members of the executive council are already cabinet ministers.

22. C

The minority group wants to change the minds of those in the majority group (those who are not interested in a new zoo). Their best option, from among those given, would be to arrange a public meeting for debate on the issue. If people against the zoo heard different points of view, they might change their minds.

It would be possible to hold a referendum on the issue. Referendums can be held in areas of local government. However, as community support for building the new zoo is very low, the vast majority of voters would most likely vote no. The referendum would simply make the lack of support official. The minority group could not hold an election vote on the issue. No group can randomly organize an election that concerns a local government matter. Letters to the local newspaper might be worthwhile and effective, but they would likely not change the minds of people to the extent that presenting both sides of the issue in a debate could.

23. B

The given information states that the letter writer thinks the town must build the recreation centre. Whether that is actually the case, the letter writer believes their viewpoint is correct.

The letter writer argues that the local government should pay for the recreation centre. The idea of people raising money to build recreation centres is not mentioned. Although the letter writer states that municipal governments must meet people's needs for recreation, this may or may not be correct. This may be the writer's opinion. The letter writer is not necessarily making a statement of fact.

24. C

Associations such as the ACFA, the MNAA, and the FNA do not have the ability to draft or create laws; bylaws are created by Métis and First Nations local governments, and provincial laws are created in the legislative assembly of the Alberta government.

Associations such as the ACFA, the MNAA, and the FNA do work toward protecting the rights of their members, and preserving their members' culture and identity. They act as a voice to support their members' interests.

25. A

The best way to find out what most people are thinking is to conduct a survey. A properly conducted survey will give a great deal of information about what many people are thinking.

Talking to people is always useful. However, it can be very time-consuming to talk to more than a few people. A survey allows feedback from a greater number of people. Advertisements would only reach some people. Also, only the people with strong opinions might respond. Media reports may or may not be accurate, and such reports would not necessarily give the viewpoints of most citizens living in a community.

Historical Models of Democracy

HISTORICAL MODELS OF DEMOCRACY

Table of Correlations			
Specific Expectation	**Practice Questions**	**Unit Test Questions**	**Practice Test**
Students will:			
6.2.3 *Analyze the structure and functions of the democratic system in ancient Athens by exploring and reflecting upon the following questions and issues:*			
6.2.3.1 How was the government of ancient Athens structured?	1, 2, 3, 4, 5	1, 2, 3, 4	28, 29
6.2.3.2 How did the structure of the government in ancient Athens provide opportunities for citizens to participate in decision-making?			46, 47
6.2.3.3 How did identity, status, and class structure impact citizenship in ancient Athens?	6, 7, 8	5, 6, 7	30, 31
6.2.3.4 How did the social structure of ancient Athens impact its political structure?	10	8	32, 33, 34, 35, 36
6.2.3.5 To what extent were democratic ideals of equity and fairness part of the structure of government and society in ancient Athens?	9		WR3
6.2.4 *Analyze the structure and functions of the Iroquois Confederacy by exploring and reflecting upon the following questions and issues:*			
6.2.4.1 How was the Iroquois Confederacy structured?	11, 12	9, 10, 11, 14, 18	37
6.2.4.2 What was the role and status of men and women within the Iroquois Confederacy?	14	12	38, 39, 40, 41
6.2.4.3 What are the advantages and disadvantages of consensus as a decision-making model for government?	15		42
6.2.4.4 How did the Six Nations use the consensus-building process?	16, 17, 18	13, 15	43, 44
6.2.4.5 How did the Wampum Belt address collective identity?	19	17	
6.2.4.6 How did the social structure of the Iroquois Confederacy impact its political structure?	13, 20	16	45
6.2.4.7 To what extent did the decision-making process within the Iroquois Confederacy reflect democratic ideals of equity and fairness?			WR3

HISTORICAL MODELS OF DEMOCRACY

6.2.3.1 How was the government of ancient Athens structured?

THE STRUCTURE OF THE GOVERNMENT OF ANCIENT ATHENS

In ancient times, Greece was not a unified country as it is today. There was no federal Greek government, and the Greek people often warred among themselves. Instead, ancient Greece was ruled by several independent city states. A city state is a city that makes its own laws and does not answer to a higher government. These city states often controlled nearby villages, which made it easier for them to get food, cloth, and other goods.

One of the strongest city states of ancient Greece was Athens. Athens controlled the region of Attica in the southeast. It was a rich city with a strong army. Before 510 BCE, Athens was controlled by kings and tyrants. After 510 BCE, Athens became a democracy: the government was in the hands of the people.

THE ASSEMBLY

The most important government body was the Assembly. The Assembly met at the *Pnyx*—a flat, open area on the top of a hill with a platform carved into the rock. Several thousand citizens could attend meetings at the *Pnyx*, especially for important topics. Usually, at least 6 000 citizens had to be present for a vote to be legal. If attendance was too low, a slave was sent into the city with a rope covered in red paint. The slave would use the rope to mark people's clothing. Anyone with a red mark had to go to the Assembly immediately. Those who did not obey could be fined.

The Assembly met every 10 days or so. Any citizen could attend, and any citizen could propose a topic for debate. Sometimes, the matters being discussed were personal. A citizen might complain about a shopkeeper who cheated him, for example. Other times, the topics were very important. Religion, taxes, and war against another city state were popular topics.

Once the topic was debated, it was time for the vote. This was usually done by a show of hands. If it was unclear which side had the majority, voting was done using coloured stones. Citizens would put stones in a large clay jug with a pale stone for yes and a dark stone for no. Once the vote was taken, the Assembly leader would formally announce the decision.

The Council of 500

The Council of 500 was called the *boule*. The *boule* was in charge of the day-to-day operation of Athens, including the agenda for the Assembly. Any decisions that the Council made were presented to the Assembly. The Council could propose laws or changes, but the Assembly had the final say.

The Council was made up of representatives from the 10 tribes of Attica, the area that Athens ruled. Each tribe had 50 representatives who were chosen in a lottery. Any citizen in a tribe could be picked as long as he was over 30 years old. Council service lasted one year, and each tribe was in charge of the Council for one-tenth of the year. Once the year was over, a new Council was chosen.

The Council was led by a chairman, but the position only lasted for one day. Again, a lottery was used to select the chairman. This kept any one person from taking unfair advantage of the position. The chairman was assisted at all times by 50 council members in case an emergency came up.

The Courts

The Athenian justice system was run by magistrates. The magistrates, like the council members, were citizens chosen by lottery. They, too, served a one-year term. The magistrates acted as judges. If a crime was minor, the magistrate could impose a sentence after hearing the evidence. The punishment was usually a fine.

For more serious crimes, the magistrate could send the case to a jury. Any citizen over 30 could be selected for jury duty. Juries, as well, were chosen by lottery. Juries in ancient Athens were huge by today's standards—as many as 1 500 people could make up the jury for a single case. The jury listened while each side told its story. There were no lawyers.

Once the plaintiff (the accuser) and the defendant (the accused person) had made their statements, the jury would discuss the case. The verdict (decision of guilt or innocence) was reached in the same way as a decision in the Assembly in which the majority view was used. If the defendant was found guilty, the jury decided what the punishment would be.

Practice Questions: 1, 2, 3, 4, 5

6.2.3.2 How did the structure of the government in ancient Athens provide opportunities for citizens to participate in decision-making?

HOW CITIZENS OF ANCIENT ATHENS PARTICIPATED IN DECISION-MAKING

Many positions in the Athenian government were held by ordinary citizens. It did not matter if a citizen was rich or poor. Everyone had an equal chance of being elected. The use of the lottery system meant that every citizen contributed equally in Athenian government. They usually served for only a year, so no one person or group could come to control the government.

The Assembly gave all citizens the chance to be heard. It was an excellent example of direct democracy. The citizens themselves were the government. They did not elect representatives. They debated and voted on laws themselves. Any citizen could speak before the Assembly, and any citizen could propose a new law or argue against one. Also, every citizen was considered equal. In other Greek cities, wealthy people had more of a say in government than ordinary citizens. In Athens, this was not the case.

This is not to say that Athens did not have leaders. Many positions were too important to leave to a citizen lottery. For example, the *strategoi* (army and navy leaders) were not chosen by lottery. A *strategos* usually had to be wealthy because he had to pay for weapons and armour for his soldiers and build ships. The *strategoi* were elected by the Assembly for one-year terms. A popular *strategos* would be re-elected. Unfortunately, a *strategos* who lost a battle would not be re-elected and might even be punished by a jury.

In ancient Athens, the best-known leader was a *strategos* named Pericles. It was during Pericles's time as *strategos* that Athenian democracy flourished. Historians often call this time a golden age for Athens. Pericles also encouraged the arts and architecture. Today, buildings and sculptures from his time are visited by millions of tourists every year.

6.2.3.3 How did identity, status, and class structure impact citizenship in ancient Athens?

THE IMPACT OF IDENTITY, STATUS, AND CLASS STRUCTURE IN ANCIENT ATHENS

Not every person in Athens was a citizen. In fact, most people in Athens could not participate in government. Only certain people could become citizens.

The slaves were at the bottom of the social order. They were often people from other cities who had been taken prisoner during war. They were seen as property and did the boring, dangerous, or time-consuming jobs. Slaves were very common in Athens—even a poor citizen would have two or more slaves to help care for children, clean the house, and do other chores. Slaves, especially household slaves, were generally treated well. Some became like members of the family. However, they had no choice but to work and do as they were told.

Because of Athens's great wealth, many foreigners came to live there. These people were known as *metics*. The *metics* were free to work and live as they chose. They had to obey the law and pay taxes like citizens. During times of war, *metics* would even fight for Athens. They were, however, not considered to be citizens. They could not participate in the government. It was extremely rare for a *metic* to be granted citizenship because only the Assembly was able to do that. For example, if a *metic* acted heroically in battle, the people of the Assembly might vote to grant him citizenship.

Female citizens in Athens were not allowed to participate in government. In fact, women had little say in any aspect of life in Athens. They were expected to remain at home, raise children, weave clothing, and do other household tasks. The only time they left the house was to participate in religious ceremonies. A woman always had to have a male guardian to look after her and accompany her. This person was usually her father, her brother, or her husband.

Only male citizens were allowed to participate in government. To earn the right, all Athenian males had to serve in the army from ages 18 to 20. A man could not be a citizen unless both his parents were also citizens. Except in rare cases, a citizen had to be a member of one of the 10 tribes of Attica.

Practice Questions: 6, 7, 8

6.2.3.4 How did the social structure of ancient Athens impact its political structure?

THE IMPACT OF THE SOCIAL STRUCTURE OF ANCIENT ATHENS ON POLITICAL STRUCTURE

The social structure of Athens helped shape its government. The leaders of Athens felt that citizenship was a great responsibility. As a consequence, only those considered to have earned the responsibility could participate in government.

In Athens, slaves actually outnumbered citizens. If slaves could have voted, they would have run the city. Because citizens had slaves to do the work for them, they had the free time to participate in politics. Slavery helped make democracy possible. Beyond that, slaves were generally uneducated. They were only concerned with serving their owner. In Athens, slaves did not care about politics.

Even though *metics* were trusted to live and work in the city, they were still considered to be foreigners. The Athenians did not believe that foreigners would have the best interests of the city at heart. If a *metic* still had ties to his home city, his vote might be biased. In ancient Greece, no city state could afford to fully trust another. The common belief was that today's ally might be tomorrow's enemy.

Women in Athens had few rights, even by the standards of ancient Greece. Athenian girls did not learn about politics; only boys went to school. Women in Athens were kept sheltered. They rarely left their homes except to go to religious ceremonies. These ceremonies were important to the Athenians, and women must have looked forward to getting out of the house for a while. At every stage of her life, an Athenian woman's duty was to obey a man—usually her father or husband. Women were important in Athens, but their role was completely separate from politics.

Male citizens spent a lot of time in the company of other men. They went to school together, they served in the army together, and they spent long hours in the marketplace, Assembly, or workplace together. Politics was a popular topic, so male citizens always knew about the political issues of the day.

Practice Question: 10

6.2.3.5 To what extent were democratic ideals of equity and fairness part of the structure of government and society in ancient Athens?

DEMOCRATIC IDEALS AND THE STRUCTURE OF GOVERNMENT AND SOCIETY IN ANCIENT ATHENS

By today's standards, the society and politics of Athens seem unfair. Slavery was an accepted part of life in Athens. Women were closed off from politics and much of society. Immigrants to Athens could only become citizens in extremely rare circumstances. Even a man born in Athens could not become a citizen if his mother, for example, was a *metic*. In short, most of Athens's residents could not participate in government.

Athenian democracy differs from our own in many other ways. In all cases, decisions were made by majority rule. The views of the minority were not taken into account. Individuals did not have any guaranteed rights. If the decision of the majority went against a person, there was nothing the person could do about it. The best example of this was the practice of ostracism. Once a year, the Assembly could vote to exile a person and force him to leave the city. There were no rules of evidence. If enough people were against a person, then that person was thrown out of Athens.

The same applies to the courts. There were no real rules of evidence. The plaintiff and defendant had to do their best to convince the jury of their argument. Wealthy people often paid skilled speech writers to help them influence the jury's decision. Often, a person's ability to persuade was more important than the actual evidence.

By the standards of 500 BCE, Athenian politics was extremely fair and equitable. Throughout most of the world, political power was in the hands of kings and tyrants. Athens was governed by the people. Every citizen had a voice in politics, even if he was not wealthy or powerful. In more modern times, when the nations of Europe began to adopt democracy, they looked to ancient Athens as an ideal example of democratic government.

The citizens of Athens met often in the Assembly. They had a real, direct influence on government. The average Athenian man was involved in politics in a way that few people are today. He was constantly discussing and debating with his fellow citizens. He was present as laws were proposed and voted on. This hands-on experience gave Athenian citizens a real sense of the importance of democracy.

Practice Question: 9

THE ORIGIN OF THE SIX NATIONS

THE PEACEMAKER

According to the oral history of the Iroquois, they were once five tribes who constantly fought one another. One day, a Huron man named Deganawidah entered the lands of the Iroquois. He was determined to bring peace to the Iroquois. He came upon a man named Hiawatha, who was sad because an evil chief had caused his daughters to die. Deganawidah comforted Hiawatha, and Hiawatha became a follower. As Deganawidah's follower and spokesman, Hiawatha worked to unite the Iroquois tribes under the Great Law of Peace. All of the chiefs agreed, except one.

Tadodaho, the evil Onondaga chief who had caused Hiawatha such grief, was difficult to convince. Hiawatha went to Tadodaho. Even after suffering greatly at the hands of the evil chief, Hiawatha persisted and managed to convert him to peaceful ways.

Deganawidah gathered the chiefs together in Onondaga territory. The chiefs buried their weapons. On that spot, they planted the Tree of Great Peace, a symbol of the new bonds between the Iroquois nations. The Great Law of Peace had become a reality. The Great Law, called *Gayanekshagowa*, united the five warring tribes of Cayuga, Mohawk, Oneida, Onondaga, and Seneca as a Confederacy. According to the Great Law, members of the Confederacy were forbidden from attacking one another. The Great Law also established the constitution of the Confederacy, its laws, its system of government, and many of its rituals. Eventually, Tadodaho became the leader of the Iroquois people.

Because of this, Deganawidah is known as the Great Peacemaker. He and Hiawatha are remembered by the Iroquois people to this day. Tadodaho, too, is remembered: his name has now become the title for the spiritual leader of the Iroquois.

The date of the Confederacy's founding is not firmly established. Until recently, archaeologists believed that it was founded sometime in the 1500s. Some new evidence suggests that it was formed even earlier in 1142. In any event, the Confederacy was founded before European colonization of the region began.

THE NATIONS OF THE CONFEDERACY

The Iroquois nations' territory covered much of the present-day state of New York. The Iroquois travelled, traded, and warred throughout much of the North American continent. Before and during the European colonization, the Confederacy was a major power with many rivals. In fact, the name Iroquois probably comes from an insult in the language of the Algonquians, a frequent enemy of the Iroquois. They referred to the members of the Confederacy as *irinakhoiw* or real adders—an adder is a poisonous snake. To the French, who met the Algonquians early, it would have sounded like *Iroqu*, to which they added the French suffix *-ois*. The Iroquois refer to themselves as the *Haudenosaunee* or People of the Longhouse.

These are the original five nations of the Confederacy from east to west:

- The Mohawk or *Ganienkegaga* were known as People of the Great Flint. The name Mohawk is also likely to have come from an Algonquian insult: *Mohowawog* (man-eaters).

- The Oneida or *Onayotekaono* were known as People of the Upright Stone. In the early 1700s, the Oneida hosted the Tuscarora tribe of North Carolina, who had been driven from their lands by European settlers.

- The Onondaga or *Onundagaono* were known as People of the Hills. As the central nation of the Confederacy, the Onondaga hosted the Haudenosaunee Grand Council.

- The Cayuga or *Guyohkohnyoh* were known as People of the Great Swamp. Most of the Cayuga live in Canada today. They were nearly wiped out during the American War of Independence.

- The Seneca or *Onondowahgah* were known as People of the Great Hill. The Seneca took their name from their capital, Osininka.

The Tuscarora or *Ska-ruh-reh*, known as Shirt-Wearers, became the sixth nation of the Confederacy in 1720, after being sponsored by the Oneida. The Oneida and Onondaga gave them land to settle on.

The Clans

In addition to belonging to a nation, Iroquois people belong to a clan. The clans are named after animals, such as the deer, heron, turtle, hawk, or wolf. Members of the same clan are considered family, even if they belong to different nations. The clans are lead by the clan mothers.

The position of clan mother is hereditary and is passed from mother to daughter. Clan mothers have the right to select and remove chiefs. They select men who are most likely to live up to the Great Law of Peace. If a chief commits a crime, ignores the wishes of the people, or violates the Great Law, the clan mother can remove him from office. She can then give the title of chief to another man.

The Chiefs

There are 50 chiefs in the Iroquois Confederacy. Together, these chiefs make up the Grand Council, which discusses topics that are important to the Iroquois people. They use a formal process of consensus decision-making. In their decisions, the chiefs must follow the Great Law. They must also consider the long-term effects of their decisions. If a decision will harm future generations, it is considered to be a bad decision. Clan mothers select chiefs who are wise, respected, and kind members of the community.

Each original member of the Confederacy has a set number of chiefs on the Grand Council. The Onondaga, who host the Grand Council, have 14 chiefs. The Cayuga have 10. The Mohawk and Oneida have 9 each, and the Seneca have 8. Having more chiefs does not give a nation more power or influence. There is no possibility, for example, of the Onondaga outvoting the Seneca simply because they have more chiefs. A nation's number of chiefs is based on the number of clans within that nation.

Tadodaho, the Iroquois spiritual leader, acts as the chairman of the Grand Council. He is selected from among the Onondaga chiefs. In addition to his ceremonial role, Tadodaho acts as the Confederacy's voice when it addresses other peoples. If a decision of the Council affects another nation, like Canada or the United States, it is Tadodaho who informs the nation.

In addition to the Council chiefs, there were two other types of chiefs: war chiefs and pine tree chiefs. War chiefs advised the Council during times of war. They also carried out the military orders of the Council and organized war bands. Finally, if the Grand Council became corrupt or ignored the people, the war chiefs could remove them by force, if necessary. There were five war chiefs, one for each of the original Five Nations. The pine tree chiefs were men gifted in the particular areas of diplomacy, organization, and trading. The war and pine tree chiefs were selected by the Grand Council.

Practice Questions: 11, 12

6.2.4.2 What was the role and status of men and women within the Iroquois Confederacy?

THE ROLE AND STATUS OF MEN AND WOMEN IN THE IROQUOIS CONFEDERACY

In the Confederacy, men and women had traditional roles. Men were responsible for hunting, fishing, fighting, and cutting down trees to build canoes and longhouses. The longhouses were huge buildings that housed many families. Although they had the Great Peace, the Iroquois often fought against other First Nations. They fought to defend themselves, to expand their territory, or later, to control the valuable fur trade with the Europeans. The nations of the Confederacy, however, did not fight one another.

Iroquois men rarely worked alone. They relied upon one another to accomplish their goals. They did not go hunting by themselves, but in large hunting parties. These hunting parties would split up into groups. One group would scare the animals by making lots of noise. The animals would panic and run from the hunters—straight toward the other group that was waiting for them.

An Iroquois man worked for the benefit of his community, not just for himself or his family. Any profit from hunting or trade went to the community. Even powerful men, such as chiefs, were not rich. The village, clan, and nation were more important than the individual.

Iroquois women had more freedom and responsibility than women in most other societies. They tended the crops and the children. They were in charge of the croplands and the longhouses. When a Iroquois couple married, the man would live in his wife's longhouse. Children were born into the mother's clan.

Like the men, women worked with one another for the good of the village. They planted and irrigated the crops. The Iroquois grew beans, corn, and squash. These three crops were so important to the Iroquois that they called them the Three Sisters and held celebrations to honour them. Iroquois women also did the cooking and made all the clothing.

Although Iroquois men and women had separate and well-defined roles, they were equals in society. They were also political equals. They relied upon one another for the good of the village, clan, nation, and Confederacy.

Practice Question: 14

6.2.4.3 What are the advantages and disadvantages of consensus as a decision-making model for government?

CONSENSUS AS A DECISION-MAKING MODEL FOR GOVERNMENT

Consensus decision-making means that decisions are not made unless everyone agrees. Issues are debated and discussed until everyone agrees on a course of action. Consensus decision-making is relatively rare for governments. In most democracies, decisions are made according to a majority vote. Because the representatives belong to different political parties, regions, and so forth, consensus in a democracy is difficult to achieve.

Consensus works well for decisions made in small groups. It requires the participants to be open-minded and to consider the view of the minority. Everyone's opinion matters, not just the majority view. Consensus also encourages members to put the interests of the group ahead of their own interests. This means that individuals must be willing to compromise and change their views to be more in line with the group. A good consensus meets everyone's needs, and everyone has a say in the decision-making process.

On the other hand, if a person cannot or will not compromise, consensus becomes impossible. It can be difficult, even when people are open-minded, to find a solution that is acceptable to everyone. The more people who are involved, the less likely consensus becomes. This means that a government has to find a balance. Too few people and the consensus will not represent everyone. Too many people and consensus becomes difficult, if not impossible. Consensus requires a lot of time and discussion to achieve.

Practice Question: 15

6.2.4.4 How did the Six Nations use the consensus-building process?

THE SIX NATIONS AND THE CONSENSUS-BUILDING PROCESS

The Grand Council was not the sole decision-making body of the Six Nations. Most of the time, issues were discussed and resolved locally. In these discussions, people tried to reach a consensus, often with the advice of the clan mothers and the faithkeepers. The faithkeepers had an important ceremonial role among the Iroquois—they led Iroquois rituals for such events as weddings, funerals, and religious celebrations. Once the people had reached a consensus, the clan mother would inform the clan's chief of the decision.

For serious matters, especially those that affected the whole Confederacy, the people would turn to the Grand Council. First, someone would inform the Onondaga chiefs of the issue or proposal. This would often be a clan mother. The Onondaga were the fire-keepers: it was their responsibility to host the council meetings. They invited the rest of the chiefs to the Council. Once the chiefs were present, the Onondaga welcomed them to the Council and thanked them for attending.

The Council would then elect a spokesman for the day. This spokesman would be a chief from the Onondaga, Mohawk, or Seneca nations. He was responsible for making sure that the Council meeting went according to the rules of the Great Law. There was a specific process to follow.

Once the spokesman announced the issue, the chiefs of the Mohawk and Seneca would quietly discuss it among themselves. These two nations were called the Elder Brothers since they were the first two nations to join the Confederacy. They would discuss the issue until they reached a consensus. They would tell the chiefs of the Oneida and Cayuga, the Younger Brothers, of their decision. The Younger Brothers would hold their own discussion, and again, they worked to reach a consensus.

If the Oneida and Cayuga agreed with the Mohawk and Seneca, they would ask the Onondaga to confirm the decision. The Mohawk would announce it to the Council. This was done, in part, to ensure that the decision was the one they had agreed on. Having agreed, the chiefs and clan mothers would act on the decision. The only exception was for declarations of war or treaties— if enough clan mothers objected to the decision, it was overruled.

If the Oneida and Cayuga could not agree with the Mohawk and Seneca, they would inform the Onondaga. The Onondaga would ask the Elder Brothers to re-examine the issue. The Elder Brothers could choose to do so, thus starting the process again, or decide to set the issue aside until they could get advice and information from their people.

At the Council, each chief was advised by a clan mother and a pair of faithkeepers. They would make sure that the chief was acting according to the Great Law of Peace and the needs of his people.

If there was a major threat to the Confederacy, each clan would hold a meeting. Everyone— men, women, and children—was allowed to speak at these meetings. Once they had reached a consensus, the clan mother would tell the chief. The chief would then inform the other chiefs of his nation, and the chiefs together would tell the Grand Council.

Practice Questions: 16, 17, 18

6.2.4.5 How did the Wampum Belt address collective identity?

WAMPUM BELT AND THE COLLECTIVE IDENTITY

Wampum held a special place in Iroquois ceremonies. Wampum beads, made of purple and white shells, were strung together or woven into belts. Wampum strings were used for several purposes. Clan mothers carried special wampum strings to show their status. A person might carry a wampum string to remember a loved one. War chiefs had a black wampum string. If the Grand Council became corrupt, the war chiefs would bring the black wampum to the Council as a warning to the Grand Chiefs.

Wampum belts were created to symbolize treaties and to tell stories from Iroquois history. Each belt had a specific texture that a skilled wampum keeper could read by running his hands along it. One important wampum belt is the Two Row Wampum, which records a treaty between the Iroquois and the Dutch in 1613. The belt depicts two purple stripes side by side on a white background. The white represents a river—the river of peace and respect. The two stripes represent an Iroquois canoe and a Dutch ship sailing side by side. This symbolizes that each nation has its own laws and customs, and they will not interfere with one another. It also shows that the Iroquois saw (and still see) themselves as a single, unified group. There is one broad stripe representing the Iroquois, not five thin ones.

The most sacred wampum belt is the Hiawatha Wampum. This belt records the Great Law of Peace and the foundation of the Confederacy. The flag of the Confederacy, in fact, is a reproduction of the Hiawatha Wampum. The white tree in the centre represents the Tree of Great Peace. It is also the symbol of the Onondaga nation, which hosts the Grand Council. The four squares represent the other four nations who first adopted the Great Law of Peace. The squares are connected by a white line, which shows how the nations are interconnected. Another white line—the Path of Peace—extends to the borders of the wampum belt. This means that other nations are welcome on the Path.

These belts show that, although the Iroquois come from different nations, they are politically, socially, and culturally united.

Practice Question: 19

6.2.4.6 How did the social structure of the Iroquois Confederacy impact its political structure?

THE SOCIAL STRUCTURE OF THE IROQUOIS CONFEDERACY

In Iroquois society, men and women were considered equals. They had, however, separate and clearly defined roles. Men hunted and fished; women farmed and made clothing. Both men and women helped the community in their own ways. The Iroquois political system was similar.

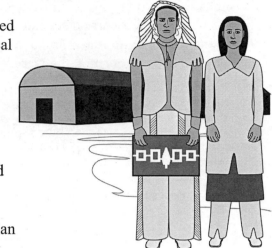

Only men could become chiefs, although this has changed in modern times. Only women could become clan mothers. The relationship between the chiefs and the clan mothers was complex and ensured that no gender dominated the other. The only way a man could become a chief was to be chosen by a clan mother. On the other hand, the only way a clan mother had a voice in the Grand Council was through the chief. A clan mother had the authority to remove a chief from power, but a clan mother who abused her power could have her authority revoked by the Council. The two major powers in Iroquois society were kept in balance. If a person from one group did not obey the Great Law, the other group could remove him or her from power.

The Grand Council system ensured each nation had an equal voice. No nation could dominate another nation. In order for a decision to become law, all of the nations had to agree to it. The presence of the clan mothers and faithkeepers ensured that the chiefs worked in the best interests of the people. The chiefs could not ignore the will of the nation or the Great Law.

An Iroquois citizen worked for the good of the group—the longhouse, village, clan, or nation. Citizens rarely worked by themselves; instead, they worked in teams to accomplish their goals. This sense of community carried over into the Iroquois political system. All decisions from local matters to issues affecting the whole Confederacy were made by consensus.

Practice Questions: 13, 20

6.2.4.7 To what extent did the decision-making process within the Iroquois Confederacy reflect democratic ideals of equity and fairness?

THE IROQUOIS CONFEDERACY AND THE DEMOCRATIC IDEALS OF EQUITY AND FAIRNESS

The Confederacy was not a democracy. Neither the clan mothers nor the chiefs were elected by the people. The position of clan mother was hereditary, and the chiefs were appointed by the clan mothers. In both cases, the people had no real say in who their leaders would be. Also, despite the remarkable gender equality in Iroquois society, men had a political advantage. A man who was seen as hard-working, honest, and respectful of the Great Law could hope to become a faithkeeper, a council chief, a war chief, or a pine tree chief. A woman, on the other hand, had no such hope. Unless she was directly related to a clan mother, there was practically no chance of her becoming a clan mother herself one day.

The Confederacy, however, achieved a level of fairness and equity that was unmatched at the time. Iroquois women participated in politics centuries before women won the right to vote in modern democracies. At the local level, everyone's voice mattered. Even a child's opinion would be taken into consideration. Foreigners who swore to live by the Great Peace could become part of a nation. Even people captured in war could be adopted by a clan and become full Iroquois citizens. The example of the Tuscarora shows that entire nations could be welcomed into the Confederacy.

The Iroquois political structure ensured that the political leaders of the Confederacy respected the will of the people and the Great Law of Peace. Because decisions were made by consensus, they had to be acceptable to everyone. This process had several positive outcomes. First, this made sure that everyone worked together in the decision-making process. Second, this ensured that the majority could not dominate the minority. Third, this meant that everyone felt included in the decision-making process. This last point is more important than it seems. Many democracies, including Canada, have seen fewer and fewer people voting in recent years. The Iroquois political structure proved that when people feel included, they are far more likely to want to participate in the process of government.

PRACTICE QUESTIONS—HISTORICAL MODELS OF DEMOCRACY

1. Which of the following phrases **best** describes the political make-up of ancient Greece?

   A. A kingdom with frequent civil wars

   B. A collection of independent city-states

   C. A loose confederation of competing provinces

   D. A republic where the strongest city became the capital

2. In which of the following places did the ancient Athenian Assembly meet?

   A. The Pnyx

   B. The Agora

   C. The Acropolis

   D. The Bouleterion

3. The role of the Council of 500 was to

   A. enforce the decisions of the Assembly

   B. approve the decisions made by the Assembly

   C. coordinate the day-to-day operation of Athens

   D. run the lotteries for important government positions

4. The Council of 500 was made up of

   A. 25 members from each of the twenty tribes of Attica

   B. 50 members from each of the ten tribes of Attica

   C. 100 members from each of the five tribes of Attica

   D. 125 members from each of the four tribes of Attica

5. The people in charge of the Athenian courts were called

   A. archons

   B. tribunes

   C. strategoi

   D. magistrates

6. Which of the following statements regarding slavery in ancient Athens is **false**?
   A. Slaves outnumbered citizens in Athens.
   B. Only wealthy citizens could afford slaves.
   C. Household slaves were usually treated well.
   D. People captured in wars could become slaves.

7. Which of the following statements **best** describes the political role of women in ancient Athens?
   A. They participated equally with men.
   B. They could only be selected for jury duty
   C. They could only participate in the Assembly.
   D. They were not allowed to participate in politics.

8. What was an Athenian woman's **main** duty?
   A. To educate her children
   B. To run the family business
   C. To obey her father or husband
   D. To cook and clean for the family

9. Which of the following statements **best** describes the practice of ostracism in ancient Athens?
   A. A jury found a person guilty of a crime.
   B. A citizen was appointed to the position of strategos.
   C. The Assembly voted to exile a person from the city.
   D. A metic became a citizen of Athens for service to the city.

10. Which of the following statements is the **most accurate** criticism of the Athenian political system?
    A. Women had to stay in their homes most of the time.
    B. Most residents of Athens could not participate in politics.
    C. Wealthy people had more political power than other citizens.
    D. Most citizens of Athens did not bother to participate in politics.

11. The Great Law of Peace was brought to the Iroquois by a Huron man named
    A. Hiawatha
    B. Tadodaho
    C. Deganawidah
    D. Thayendanegea

12. By what name do the Iroquois call themselves?
    A. Irinakhoiw
    B. Onundagaono
    C. Haudenosaunee
    D. Gayanekshagowa

13. The **most common** way for an Iroquois woman to become a clan mother was to
    A. win an election within the clan
    B. be appointed by the Grand Council
    C. be appointed by her nation's chiefs
    D. inherit the title from her own mother

14. Which of the following tasks would an Iroquois man have been **least likely** to perform?
    A. Fishing
    B. Hunting
    C. Farming
    D. Carpentry

15. Which of the following statements regarding consensus decision-making is **false**?
    A. It puts the interests of the group first.
    B. It can require a lot of time and discussion.
    C. It works best with smaller groups of people.
    D. It is a common practice in most modern democracies.

16. The number of chiefs for each nation was determined by
    A. the total population of the nation
    B. the number of clans within the nation
    C. the pre-Confederation number of chiefs
    D. the number of villages within the nation

17. Which nation hosted the Grand Council of the Iroquois?

    A. The Seneca

    B. The Oneida

    C. The Mohawk

    D. The Onondaga

Use the following information to answer the next question.

Sequence of Events at Grand Council Meetings
I. The Tuscarora, as Firekeepers, opened the meeting.
II. The Mohawk and Onondaga were the first to discuss the matter under consideration.
III. The Oneida and Cayuga were the next to discuss the matter under consideration.
IV. The council chiefs voted on the matter that had been discussed.

18. Which of the given events from the Grand Council meetings is **true**?

    A. I

    B. II

    C. III

    D. IV

19. The Two Row Wampum was created to represent

    A. a treaty with the Dutch

    B. the Great Law of Peace

    C. a traditional Iroquois legend

    D. the Five Nations of the Iroquois

20. When making a decision, a chief's most important consideration was

    A. the Great Law of Peace

    B. the wishes of the clan mother

    C. the will of his nation's people

    D. the needs of future generations

ANSWERS AND SOLUTIONS—PRACTICE QUESTIONS

1. B	5. D	9. C	13. D	17. D
2. A	6. B	10. B	14. C	18. C
3. C	7. D	11. C	15. D	19. A
4. B	8. C	12. C	16. B	20. A

1. B

Ancient Greece was a collection of independent city-states. The various city-states had the same culture, religion, and language. However, there was no central Greek government until Greece was conquered by Macedonia.

2. A

The Assembly met at the Pnyx, a large, open area just outside the city of Athens. It was on a hilltop and had a speaking platform and benches carved from the rock.

An agora is an open paved area within a city, often used as a marketplace. The Acropolis of Athens held many of the city's temples, theatres, and other great works of architecture. The Bouleterion was where the Council of 500 met.

3. C

The Council of 500 coordinated the day-to-day operation of Athens. It also prepared the agenda for meetings of the Assembly.

The Council was not responsible for enforcing the Assembly's decisions. It had no power to approve the decisions of the Assembly; the Assembly had the final say. Important government positions were normally filled by persons elected by the Assembly, not by lottery.

4. B

Attica was the area controlled by Athens. The ten tribes of Attica each had 50 citizens on the Council. These citizens were chosen by lottery.

5. D

A magistrate was a citizen chosen by lottery to serve in the court system. Magistrates had the power to decide guilt or innocence. If they could or would not, they sent the case to a jury.

The Archons ruled Athens before the rise of democracy. Tribunes were Roman political figures. Strategoi were Greek generals.

6. B

Even poor Athenian citizens would own two or more slaves. Because of this, slaves greatly outnumbered citizens. Those slaves working in Athenian households were usually treated well. They were often trusted to look after children and to help educate them. Slaves were often citizens of other city-states captured in war.

7. D

Athenian women had no political role. Only male citizens were allowed to participate in politics.

8. **C**

> **Throughout her life, an Athenian woman had to obey a male guardian. This was usually her father or husband; if she had neither, her brother could be her guardian until she married.**

> An Athenian woman might help to educate her daughters, but most education was done by slaves. Women did not run businesses. Women did the cooking or cleaning (except for wealthy women, who would have slaves to do those tasks). However, she did so as part of her duty to her father or husband.

9. **C**

> **Ostracism was the practice of voting to exile someone from the city—that is, to force that person to leave. Ostracism was usually reserved for important persons who the Assembly felt had harmed the city: a general who failed in battle, a corrupt politician, etc.**

10. **B**

> **Slaves, metics, and women were not allowed to participate in politics. This means that most of Athens's residents had no role in politics.**

> It is true that women had to stay home most of the time. However, this is a criticism of Athenian society, not Athenian politics. Wealthy people had a slight political advantage, but every vote was equal. Every citizen had the same chance to be selected for Council or court service. Athenian citizens were usually eager to participate in politics. It was a major part of their daily lives, since they could participate directly.

11. **C**

> **Deganawidah, the Peacemaker, brought the Great Law of Peace to the Iroquois.**

> His loyal follower, Hiawatha, converted the evil chief Tadodaho to the ways of peace. Thayendanegea, also called Joseph Brant, was a Mohawk war chief who fought for the British during the American Civil War.

12. **C**

> **The Iroquois call themselves "Haudenosaunee," which means "people of the longhouse."**

> "Irinakhoiw" was what the Algonquians called them; it is from this word that the French derived "Iroquois." "Onundagaono" is the Iroquois name of the Onondaga. "Gayanekshagowa" is the Iroquois word for the Great Law of Peace.

13. **D**

> **The title of clan mother was passed down from mother to daughter. If the clan mother did not have a daughter, the title would go to her closest female relative.**

> There were no elections for the position. The chiefs of the Council only intervened in rare circumstances. For example, if a clan mother committed a serious crime, they could take her title away and give it to a more deserving person.

14. **C**

> **Iroquois men did not farm. Farming was the women's task.**

15. D

Consensus decision-making is not common in modern democracies. Usually, representatives in democracies look after the needs of their region or political party first. They are unlikely to reach a consensus with one another. Therefore, most modern democracies follow the wishes of the majority.

16. B

Each nation has a certain number of clans. Within each nation, each clan is represented by one clan mother. Each clan mother can appoint one chief. Therefore, the number of chiefs is determined by the number of clans within the nation.

17. D

The Onondaga hosted the Grand Council. It was their duty to summon the Council whenever discussion was needed. They kept the meeting place clean and tended the sacred fire at the centre of the lodge. This is why the Onondaga are also called the Firekeepers.

18. C

The Oneida and Cayuga, as the Younger Brothers, were the second to discuss the matter. They would discuss whether the solution proposed by the Elder Brothers was acceptable.

The Onondaga, not the Tuscarora, were the Firekeepers. The Elder Brothers, who first discussed the matter, were the Mohawk and Seneca. The council chiefs did not vote; they tried to reach a consensus.

19. A

The Two Row Wampum represents a treaty with the Dutch from 1613. The two rows are the paths of boats: an Iroquois canoe and a Dutch ship. The wampum belt shows that the paths of the two peoples will run alongside one another on the River of Life.

20. A

In all decisions, a chief had to follow the Great Law of Peace.

The other considerations were important. However, obedience to the Great Law was always the chief's first duty. (The same obedience was required of clan mothers and faithkeepers.)

112

UNIT TEST—HISTORICAL MODELS OF DEMOCRACY

1. The Assembly of ancient Athens was made up of
   A. all the male citizens of Athens
   B. five hundred elected representatives
   C. six thousand citizens chosen by lottery
   D. a maximum of 1 500 citizens chosen by a magistrate

2. How often did the Assembly meet?
   A. Once a day
   B. Once every month
   C. Once every ten days
   D. Once every three months

3. How long did the chairman of the Council of 500 serve in his role?
   A. One day
   B. One week
   C. One month
   D. One year

4. How were people selected for jury duty in ancient Athens?
   A. They were chosen by the lawyers.
   B. They were chosen by the magistrates.
   C. They were chosen by the Council of 500.
   D. They were chosen using random lotteries.

5. Athenian women rarely left the house except to
   A. visit family and friends
   B. attend Assembly meetings
   C. go shopping in the marketplace
   D. participate in religious ceremonics

6. Which of the following statements about metics is **false**?

   A. They could not own land.

   B. They could not join the army.

   C. They could not serve on a jury.

   D. They could not participate in the Assembly.

7. If a citizen married a metic, children of the couple would have what status?

   A. The children would be metics.

   B. The children would be citizens.

   C. The children would have the same status as the father.

   D. The children would have the same status as the mother.

8. Which Greek city-state was Athens's **main** rival?

   A. Sparta

   B. Thebes

   C. Piraeus

   D. Corinth

9. Deganawidah, who brought the Great Law of Peace to the Iroquois, is called the

   A. Peacegiver

   B. Peacemaker

   C. Peacekeeper

   D. Peacebringer

10. Which of the following nations was the last to join the Iroquois Confederacy?

    A. The Seneca

    B. The Oneida

    C. The Mohawk

    D. The Tuscarora

114

11. An Iroquois man could become a chief if he
    A. won an election within his clan
    B. was appointed by a clan mother
    C. won an election within his nation
    D. was selected by the other chiefs of his nation

12. In Iroquois tradition, the Three Sisters are
    A. crops grown for food
    B. Hiawatha's daughters
    C. the sun, moon, and Earth
    D. lakes Huron, Erie, and Ontario

13. The **main** role of the faithkeepers was to
    A. preserve Iroquois culture
    B. conduct important ceremonies
    C. craft wampum strings and belts
    D. advise the Grand Council chiefs

14. How many Tuscarora chiefs were on the Grand Council?
    A. 0
    B. 7
    C. 12
    D. 14

15. At the Grand Council, the Mohawk and Seneca chiefs were called the
    A. Firekeepers
    B. Elder Brothers
    C. Chiefs of the East
    D. Guardians of the Door

16. Which of the following statements regarding the Grand Council spokesman is **false**?

    A. The spokesman only served for a day.

    B. The spokesman was an Onondaga chief.

    C. The spokesman followed the rules of the Great Law.

    D. The spokesman announced the issue to be discussed.

17. On the Hiawatha Wampum belt, the four squares represent

    A. longhouses

    B. Iroquois nations

    C. the Path of Peace

    D. the leaves of the Great Tree

18. Where are the traditional lands of the Iroquois located?

    A. The Lake Ontario area (modern-day New York)

    B. The Hudson Bay area (modern-day north Ontario)

    C. The Great Plains (modern-day Montana and Alberta)

    D. The northeast coast of Canada (modern-day Labrador)

ANSWERS AND SOLUTIONS—UNIT TEST

1. A	5. D	9. B	13. B	17. B
2. C	6. B	10. D	14. A	18. A
3. A	7. A	11. B	15. B	
4. D	8. A	12. A	16. B	

1. A

Every male citizen in Athens was allowed to participate in the Assembly.

Although a minimum of six thousand citizens was usually required for a decision, participants were not selected by lottery. The Council had 500 citizens, but they were not elected. Juries had up to 1 500 members, but they were not chosen by a magistrate.

2. C

The Assembly normally met about once every ten days.

3. A

The chairman was chosen by lottery and only served for one day. This prevented any one person from dominating the Council.

4. D

Juries were selected using the lottery system. All male citizens were eligible for the lottery.

There were no lawyers in ancient Athens. A magistrate could send a case to a jury, but he did not select the jury himself. The Council did not participate in the Athenian court system.

5. D

Athenian women usually stayed at home. However, they had important roles in religious ceremonies, which were common in ancient Greece. Women rarely visited other people's homes, even those of friends and family. Women were not allowed to attend the Assembly. Men or slaves did the shopping for the household.

6. B

Metics could and did fight for Athens. In fact, this was one of the few ways that a metic could become a citizen. If he was very brave and loyal, the Assembly could make him a citizen. Otherwise, metics enjoyed few of the rights that full citizens had. They could not own land, serve in the courts or Council, or participate in the Assembly.

7. A

To be a citizen, both a child's parents had to be citizens themselves. Because of this, citizens rarely married metics.

8. A

The city-state of Sparta was Athens's main rival. Spartans were very warlike, and Spartan boys trained to become soldiers from a very young age.

The city-state of Thebes controlled the region to the north of Athens, but they lost a lot of power in earlier wars against Persia. Piraeus was not a city-state; it was a port city in Attica that was controlled by Athens. The city-state of Corinth controlled the region between Athens and Sparta. It was a rich and powerful city, but was often dominated by Athens or Sparta.

9. B

Deganawidah is honoured in Iroquois legend as the Peacemaker.

10. D

The Tuscarora were a tribe of Iroquoian-speaking people who had emigrated to what is now North Carolina long before the Great Peace.

In the 1700s, the Tuscarora were threatened by the wave of settlement in the Carolinas. Most of the tribe chose to return to their ancestral Iroquois homeland; they became the Sixth Nation of the Iroquois.

11. B

The title of chief belonged to the clan mothers. It was theirs to give or to take away. Therefore, a man could only become chief if a clan mother granted him the title.

12. A

The Three Sisters are beans, corn, and squash. These three crops were the most important food source for the Iroquois.

13. B

The faithkeepers were men who knew the ceremonies and traditions of the Iroquois. They were trusted to conduct the important ceremonies, such as weddings and celebrations. Their role as preservers of Iroquois culture is relatively recent, and it is not their main role. Anyone could craft wampum strings or belts, although the belts would be made by skilled craftspeople. The faithkeepers did advise the chiefs, but only to ensure that the chief was following the Great Law.

14. A

There are no Tuscarora chiefs on the Grand Council. They were once represented by the Oneida. Today, they are represented by the Cayuga.

15. B

The Mohawk and Seneca nations were the first two to join the Confederacy; for this reason, they are called the Elder Brothers at Council. The Onondaga are the Firekeepers. The Seneca would not be "Chiefs of the East," since they are the westernmost nation in the Confederacy. The term "Guardians of the Door" is also a made-up title.

16. B

The spokesman could also be from the Mohawk or Seneca nations.

17. B

The four squares represent the Seneca, Cayuga, Oneida, and Mohawk nations. The fifth original nation, the Onondaga, is represented by the tree in the centre of the belt.

18. A

The traditional lands of the Iroquois extend south and east from Lake Ontario, covering most of today's New York State.

KEY Strategies for Success on Tests

KEY STRATEGIES FOR SUCCESS ON TESTS

AN OVERVIEW OF THE TEST

This section is all about the skills and strategies you need to be successful on the Grade 6 Social Studies Alberta Provincial Achievement Test. It is designed for you to use together with your classroom learning and assignments.

Finding Out About the Test

Here are some questions you may wish to discuss with your teacher to help you prepare for the Grade 6 Social Studies Alberta Provincial Achievement Test.

1.	What is the purpose of the test?	The purpose is to see how well you perform on the Knowledge and Understanding and Skills and Processes outlined in the curriculum.
2.	What do I need to know to do well on the assessment?	You need to show that you have an understanding and appreciation of the relationship between governments and citizens as they engage in the democratic process as well as an understanding and appreciation of the democratic principles used by ancient Athens and the Iroquois Confederacy.
3.	What must I bring for the test?	You must bring a pencil and an eraser.
4.	Will there be graphics?	Yes, diagrams, pictures, and illustrations.
5.	What kinds of questions are on the test?	There will be multiple-choice questions on the test.
6.	How many types of each question are there?	There will be 50 multiple-choice questions on the test.
7.	How important is this test to my final grade?	Your teacher can answer this question.

Having a good understanding of effective test taking skills can help you do well on the test. Being familiar with the question format may help you in preparing for quizzes, unit tests, or year-end tests.

TEST PREPARATION AND TEST-TAKING SKILLS

THINGS TO CONSIDER WHEN TAKING A TEST

- It is normal to feel anxious before you write a test. You can manage this anxiety by
    - thinking positive thoughts. Imagine yourself doing well on the test.
    - making a conscious effort to relax by taking several slow, deep, controlled breaths. Concentrate on the air going in and out of your body.
- Before you begin the test, ask questions if you are unsure of anything.
- Jot down key words or phrases from any instructions your teacher gives you.
- Look over the entire test to find out the number and kinds of questions on the test.
- Read each question closely and reread if necessary.
- Pay close attention to key vocabulary words. Sometimes these are bolded or italicized, and they are usually important words in the question.
- If you are putting your answers on an answer sheet, mark your answers carefully. Always print clearly. If you wish to change an answer, erase the mark completely and then ensure your final answer is darker than the one you have erased.
- Use highlighting to note directions, key words, and vocabulary that you find confusing or that are important to answering the question.
- Double-check to make sure you have answered everything before handing in your test.

When taking tests, students often overlook the easy words. Failure to pay close attention to these words can result in an incorrect answer. One way to avoid this is to be aware of these words and to underline, circle, or highlight them while you are taking the test.

Even though some words are easy to understand, they can change the meaning of the entire question, so it is important that you pay attention to them. Here are some examples.

All	Always	Most likely	Probably	Best	Not
Difference	Usually	Except	Most	Unlikely	Likely

Example

1. During the race, Susan is **most likely** feeling
    A. sad
    B. weak
    C. scared
    D. determined

HELPFUL STRATEGIES FOR ANSWERING MULTIPLE-CHOICE QUESTIONS

A multiple-choice question gives you some information, and then asks you to select an answer from four choices. Each question has one correct answer. The other answers are distractors, which are incorrect. Below are some strategies to help you when answering multiple-choice questions.

- Quickly skim through the entire test. Find out how many questions there are and plan your time accordingly.

- Read and reread questions carefully. Underline key words and try to think of an answer before looking at the choices.

- If there is a graphic, look at the graphic, read the question, and go back to the graphic. Then, you may want to underline the important information from the question.

- Carefully read the choices. Read the question first and then each answer that goes with it.

- When choosing an answer, try to eliminate those choices that are clearly wrong or do not make sense.

- Some questions may ask you to select the best answer. These questions will always include words like best, most appropriate, or most likely. All of the answers will be correct to some degree, but one of the choices will be better than the others in some way. Carefully read all four choices before choosing the answer you think is the best.

- If you do not know the answer, or if the question does not make sense to you, it is better to guess than to leave it blank.

- Do not spend too much time on any one question. Make a mark (*) beside a difficult question and come back to it later. If you are leaving a question to come back to later, make sure you also leave the space on the answer sheet, if you are using one.

- Remember to go back to the difficult questions at the end of the test; sometimes clues are given throughout the test that will provide you with answers.

- Note any negative words like no or not and be sure your choice fits the question.

- Before changing an answer, be sure you have a very good reason to do so.

- Do not look for patterns on your answer sheet, if you are using one.

HELPFUL STRATEGIES FOR ANSWERING OPEN-RESPONSE QUESTIONS

A written response requires you to respond to a question or directive such as **explain**, **predict**, **list**, **describe**, **show your work**, **solve**, or **calculate.** In preparing for open-response tasks you may wish to:

- Read and reread the question carefully.

- Recognize and pay close attention to directing words such as explain, show your work, and describe.

- Underline key words and phrases that indicate what is required in your answer, such as explain, estimate, answer, calculate, or show your work.

- Write down rough, point-form notes regarding the information you want to include in your answer.

- Think about what you want to say and organize information and ideas in a coherent and concise manner within the time limit you have for the question.

- Be sure to answer every part of the question that is asked.

- Include as much information as you can when you are asked to explain your thinking.

- Include a picture or diagram if it will help to explain your thinking.

- Try to put your final answer to a problem in a complete sentence to be sure it is reasonable.

- Reread your response to ensure you have answered the question.

- Think: does your answer make sense

- Listen: does it sound right?

- Use appropriate subject vocabulary and terms in your response.

TEST PREPARATION COUNTDOWN

If you develop a plan for studying and test preparation, you will perform well on tests.

Here is a general plan to follow seven days before you write a test.

Countdown: 7 Days before the Test

1. Use "Finding Out About the Test" to help you make your own personal test preparation plan.

2. Review the following information:
   - areas to be included on the test
   - types of test items
   - general and specific test tips

3. Start preparing for the test at least 7 days before the test. Develop your test preparation plan and set time aside to prepare and study.

Countdown: 6, 5, 4, 3, 2 Days before the Test

1. Review old homework assignments, quizzcs, and tests.

2. Rework problems on quizzes and tests to make sure you still know how to solve them.

3. Correct any errors made on quizzes and tests.

4. Review key concepts, processes, formulas, and vocabulary.

5. Create practice test questions for yourself and then answer them. Work out many sample problems.

Countdown: The Night before the Test

1. The night before the test is for final preparation, which includes reviewing and gathering material needed for the test before going to bed.

2. Most important is getting a good night's rest and knowing you have done everything possible to do well on the test.

Test Day

1. Eat a healthy and nutritious breakfast.

2. Ensure you have all the necessary materials.

3. Think positive thoughts: "I can do this." "I am ready." "I know I can do well."

4. Arrive at your school early so you are not rushing, which can cause you anxiety and stress.

SUMMARY OF HOW TO BE SUCCESSFUL DURING A TEST

You may find some of the following strategies useful for writing a test.

- Take two or three deep breaths to help you relax.

- Read the directions carefully and underline, circle, or highlight any important words.

- Look over the entire test to understand what you will need to do.

- Budget your time.

- Begin with an easy question, or a question you know you can answer correctly, rather than following the numerical question order of the test.

- If you cannot remember how to answer a question, try repeating the deep breathing and physical relaxation activities first. Then, move on to visualization and positive self-talk to get yourself going.

- When answering a question with graphics (pictures, diagrams, tables, or graphs), look at the question carefully.
  - Read the title of the graphic and any key words.
  - Read the test question carefully to figure out what information you need to find in the graphic.
  - Go back to the graphic to find the information you need.

- Write down anything you remember about the subject on the reverse side of your test paper. This activity sometimes helps to remind you that you do know something and you are capable of writing the test.

- Look over your test when you have finished and double-check your answers to be sure you did not forget anything.

NOTES

PRACTICE TEST

Use the following information to answer the next three questions.

Situation I

Chung is thinking about the elections for his school's student council. He could vote for Alicia, who has a lot of good ideas about how to improve the school's music program. However, Prasad made a great speech about community involvement. Finally, there is Tyler, who is a big supporter of the school's sports teams.

Situation II

The students of Ms. Ebadi's class have decided to put on a play to raise money for charity. The only question left is to choose the charity they will give the money to. They have narrowed it down to three choices: the local animal shelter, the Food Bank, and an international charity for poor children in Africa. Each student gets to vote for the charity they prefer, and the money will go to the charity that gets the most votes.

Situation III

Lata is excited. She and her brothers all received great marks in school this year. As a reward, her parents are going to take the children to an event of their choice. Their choices include going to the zoo, to a play, or to a football game. The choice is up to Lata and her brothers, but all three children have to agree on the event. Lata plans to talk it over with her brothers after dinner.

Situation IV

Friday is going to be a special day for Ms. Westerlund's class because she has arranged for her class to go on a field trip to a Cree village. In the morning, they will learn about Cree culture and history. For lunch, they will try some traditional Cree dishes. In the afternoon, the children of the village are going to perform a ceremonial dance. The students cannot wait for Friday to arrive.

---

1. Which of the given situations is an example of direct democracy?

   A. Situation I

   B. Situation II

   C. Situation III

   D. Situation IV

2. Which of the given situations is the **least** democratic?

   A. Situation I

   B. Situation II

   C. Situation III

   D. Situation IV

3. Which of the given situations **most closely** resembles Canada's political system?

   A. Situation I

   B. Situation II

   C. Situation III

   D. Situation IV

Use the following information to answer the next three questions.

FIGMENTON, AB: A local group, the Alberta First Coalition (AFC), is concerned about the number of immigrants coming to the city from other provinces. "Albertan jobs should be going to Albertans," said AFC leader Robert Jones. "Also, the influx of people from other provinces is putting a real strain on the town's resources. We will ask the government to limit immigration from these provinces."

However, a prominent Figmenton lawyer, Jaroslav Jezek, doubts the group will succeed. "Such a law would violate the Canadian Charter of Rights and Freedoms," said Jezek.

4. The law proposed by the AFC would violate the immigrants'

   A. legal rights

   B. equality rights

   C. mobility rights

   D. democratic rights

5. If the Alberta government were to pass a law limiting immigration from the other provinces, it would be overturned by the

   A. prime minister

   B. Supreme Court

   C. Governor General

   D. lieutenant-governor

Use the following additional information to answer the next question.

> Many people in Figmenton are outraged at the attitude of the AFC. "I am disgusted that anyone could be so hostile toward fellow Canadians," said Marie Beauchamp, a local businesswoman. "They are damaging the reputation of our city! I think that the AFC should be fined or even disbanded by the provincial government."

6. Can the provincial government legally fine or disband the AFC?

   A. No, because AFC members have the right to free speech.

   B. Yes, because AFC members are abusing the right to free speech.

   C. No, because the provincial government does not interpret the Charter.

   D. Yes, because the provincial government can interpret the Charter as it wishes.

7. The purpose of the Treaty of La Grand Paix de Montréal was to

   A. cede the land near Montréal to the French

   B. make peace between warring First Nations

   C. end the war between the Haudenosaunee and the French

   D. establish trade between the Haudenosaunee and the French

8. The Treaty of La Grand Paix de Montréal was significant to relations between the Aboriginal and non-Aboriginal people of the area because it

   A. forced the Aboriginal people to forfeit their lands to non-Aboriginals

   B. highlighted the opposing worldviews of Aboriginals and non-Aboriginals

   C. showed a great deal of respect for Aboriginal collective identity and rights

   D. demonstrated the non-Aboriginal view that European values were superior

9. The Canadian Charter of Rights and Freedoms is entrenched in the Canadian Constitution, which means that

  A. it only applies to federal laws and decisions

  B. the government can never change the Charter

  C. Charter rights and freedoms are essential laws

  D. only Canadian citizens benefit from the Charter

Use the following information to answer the next two questions.

> At the Figmenton mayoral debate, there were four candidates. The candidates were asked to briefly summarize their priorities for the growing city.
>
> **Candidate I**
>
> In order to reduce traffic and pollution, I think that it is important to encourage people to take the bus more often. We will advertise public transit as an affordable, clean, safe, and convenient way for people to get around the city.
>
> **Candidate II**
>
> Unfortunately, a growing population brings a growing crime problem. If elected, I will work to increase the number of officers in the Figmenton Police Service, and I will make sure the police have the resources they need to do their jobs.
>
> **Candidate III**
>
> As our city grows, the strain on our healthcare system increases. We need to hire more doctors, nurses, and other healthcare professionals. We may even need to build new healthcare facilities to accommodate all the new people.
>
> **Candidate IV**
>
> Figmenton is a beautiful city, but littering and vandalism are becoming problems. No one wants to see garbage on the sidewalks, cigarette butts everywhere, and graffiti on the walls. If elected, I promise to tackle this problem as soon as possible.

10. Which candidate's plan will **most likely** require a new bylaw?

  A. Candidate I

  B. Candidate II

  C. Candidate III

  D. Candidate IV

11. Which candidate is **least likely** to be able to deliver on his or her campaign promises?

A. Candidate I

B. Candidate II

C. Candidate III

D. Candidate IV

Use the following information to answer the next two questions.

Monique's family has just moved from Montréal to Figmenton. Her parents want her to attend a school where classes are taught in French. There are two choices. One is École des Prairies, which has a strong French immersion program. The other choice is École St. Jacques, a Catholic school where all instruction is in French.

12. École des Prairies is **most likely** run by a

A. public school board

B. private school board

C. separate school board

D. Francophone school board

13. The curriculum at École St. Jacques is **most likely** determined by the

A. school

B. school board

C. municipal government

D. provincial government

Use the following information to answer the next five questions.

Reuven Weinberg is proud to be serving in the Alberta legislature. As a member of the Legislative Assembly, he can make a real difference for the people of South Figmenton. His constituents are worried about the increasing amount of pollution in the Little Red River, which provides water for the district. He has worked hard on a bill that would protect the river from pollution. He has also been an important part of the committee that examined the bill. He is sure it will work, and he is also sure that industries can adapt to the new law. He smiles to himself as he heads for the Chamber, which is where the Legislative Assembly meets. He is sure that the opposition MLAs will have plenty of tough questions for him!

14. Mr. Weinberg's committee that examined the bill is **mostly likely** overseen by

   A. Mr. Weinberg

   B. a cabinet minister

   C. an executive council

   D. the lieutenant-governor

15. Mr. Weinberg's bill is **most likely** being prepared for its

   A. first reading

   B. second reading

   C. third reading

   D. fourth reading

16. Mr Weinberg's bill can become a law only after it

   A. is approved by the premier

   B. is signed by the lieutenant-governor

   C. has been reviewed by the Supreme Court

   D. has received a majority vote in the legislature

17. Mr. Weinberg's responsibilities as an MLA do **not** include

   A. keeping his constituents informed about government issues and decisions

   B. trying to resolve any problems his constituents may have with the government

   C. informing the appropriate government department of his constituents' concerns

   D. making sure that appropriate government services are available in his constituency

18. Mr. Weinberg is **most likely** a member of the

    A. Alberta Liberal Party

    B. Alberta New Democratic Party

    C. Wildrose Alliance Party of Alberta

    D. Progressive Conservative Association of Alberta

Use the following information to answer the next three questions.

FIGMENTON, AB: A proposed, major highway development is creating quite a stir in Figmenton. The development, slated to begin construction next year, will see a new four lane highway run through the city, allowing for faster travel between the major cities of Glaracy and Fort Albert. The Organization of Alberta Motorists (OAM) is hailing the new highway as "essential" for quick and convenient travel in the province. The Figmenton Business Alliance (FBA) is also thrilled. "This highway means more jobs, more tourism, and more business coming to our city," said FBA leader Calvin Liao. "We've been asking for this development for a long time. Now, Figmenton will become an economic powerhouse."

However, not everyone agrees. In fact, a new group, the Figmenton Homeowners' Association (FHA), has formed to protest the development. "Any property near the highway will plummet in value," said Marthe Schmidt, the FHA president. "We'll have to put up with construction noise, and noise and pollution from all the traffic once the highway is finished."

The president of the Alberta Environmental Protection Foundation (AEP), Roberta Szarko, agrees. "The government has not considered the impact this will have on local wildlife and natural environments. The long-term damage could be drastic."

19. The Figmenton Business Alliance is a

    A. lobby group

    B. grassroots organization

    C. government department

    D. non-governmental organization

20. The Figmenton Homeowners' Association is a

    A. lobby group

    B. grassroots organization

    C. government department

    D. non-governmental organization

21. The group **least likely** to receive support from areas outside Figmenton is the

    A. Figmenton Business Alliance

    B. Organization of Alberta Motorists

    C. Figmenton Homeowners Association

    D. Alberta Environmental Protection Foundation

22. The Association canadienne-française de l'Alberta has worked toward all of the following accomplishments **except** the

    A. delivery of government services in French

    B. development of French immersion programs

    C. promotion of French-Canadian culture in Alberta

    D. introduction of French-language radio and television

23. Canada's First Nations lost most of their rights with the onset of the

    A. Constitution Act, 1867

    B. Constitution Act, 1982

    C. Royal Proclamation, 1763

    D. Treaty of La Grand Paix de Montréal, 1701

24. Services for Alberta's First Nations are run by groups known as
    A. boards
    B. councils
    C. authorities
    D. committees

25. Who are the Métis?
    A. Inhabitants of the Arctic region of Canada
    B. Persons of mixed Aboriginal and European ancestry
    C. Aboriginal persons from the United States who immigrated to Canada
    D. Persons of European ancestry who chose to adopt aboriginal customs

26. The Métis were first recognized as an Aboriginal group under the
    A. Constitution Act, 1867
    B. Constitution Act, 1982
    C. Royal Proclamation, 1763
    D. Treaty of La Grand Paix de Montréal, 1701

27. Which of the following methods is the **least effective** manner for MLAs to keep their constituents informed?
    A. Mailing newsletters to constituents
    B. Maintaining offices in their constituencies
    C. Developing a website that constituents can visit
    D. Delivering regular television or radio interviews

Use the following information to answer the next seven questions.

Phostes was making his way through the busy agora when he spotted a familiar face. "Ephialtes!" he called. His friend turned and squeezed through the crowd to shake his hand.

"Phostes, old friend, you're looking well! A little tired, though. Are things busy at your shop?"

"Actually, I'm serving as a magistrate this year. I thought it would be easy at first, but now I pray daily for Athena to grant me wisdom," replied Phostes, rubbing his tired eyes.

"Well, it's an important job."

"That it is. But you're looking pretty happy! How are things?"

Ephialtes grinned. "Excellent. I just sold a load of olive oil to a *metic* from Corinth. I made a great profit too!"

"Really? Corinthians are usually tough bargainers," said Phostes.

"This one was too busy bending my ear about the Spartan advance on Megara."

"Ah. And what did he think about it?"

"Well, he was singing Athens's praises and cursing the wicked Spartans. I'm sure if he was in Sparta, he'd be doing the opposite."

Phostes laughed. "Of course. Who knows what foreigners really think?"

Ephialtes shrugged. "Well, what do *you* think? Should we let the Spartans have Megara, or should we fight them?"

The two friends debated and argued, enjoying themselves greatly. They were deep in conversation when, all of a sudden, a red-dyed rope snaked out and lashed across their garments. Startled, the two men jumped and looked at the red mark on their clothes. The slave who held the rope was careful not to laugh at their surprise.

"Have we really been at it that long?" asked Ephialtes in amazement. "I lost track of time!"

"So much for a quiet dinner with the wife," Phostes sighed as the rope-wielding slave moved on.

"Your wife won't be home until late, remember?"

"You're right. I had forgotten. Well, come on. Let's go to the Pnyx."

"Yes, I'm looking forward to it. Hey, do you think that Pericles will be there?"

"Pericles? Of course! Wild horses couldn't keep him away, especially today!"

28. As a magistrate, Phostes's job was to

    A. conduct religious ceremonies

    B. make judgements in a law court

    C. enforce the will of the Assembly

    D. help prepare the Assembly's agenda

29. Which of the following statements about Sparta is **false**?

    A. Sparta is west of Athens.

    B. Sparta was militarily weaker than Athens.

    C. Sparta was Athens's main rival in Greece.

    D. Sparta and Athens often fought one another.

30. In ancient Greece, *metics* were

    A. messengers

    B. war captives

    C. foreign residents

    D. travelling merchants

31. This conversation suggests that Athenians generally viewed *metics* with

    A. fear

    B. hatred

    C. mistrust

    D. admiration

32. The slave struck Phostes and Ephialtes with the dyed rope because they were

    A. being selected for jury duty

    B. loitering too long in the agora

    C. violating Athens's curfew law

    D. being summoned to the Assembly

33. Phostes and Ephialtes wanted to go to the Pnyx because the Pnyx was where
- **A.** the Assembly met
- **B.** Athenians had their homes
- **C.** Athens's theatres were located
- **D.** the great temples of Athens were located

34. Ephialtes knew that Phostes's wife would not be home. Which of the following statements **best** describes why Phostes's wife was not home?
- **A.** She was attending a meeting of the Assembly.
- **B.** She was participating in a religious ceremony.
- **C.** She was gathering crops in Athens's farmlands.
- **D.** She was running Phostes's shop while he was busy.

35. Pericles was a prominent Athenian
- **A.** priest
- **B.** general
- **C.** magistrate
- **D.** philosopher

36. The final decision about war against Sparta would be made by the
- **A.** Pericles
- **B.** Council
- **C.** generals
- **D.** Assembly

Use the following information to answer the next six questions.

The worried Mohawk villagers were gathered around the central fire. This year's harvest was poor. And, as if that weren't serious enough, the Algonquin had raided Mohawk lands. They had taken much of the corn, beans, and squash the villagers would need to last through the coming winter.

"I have heard from the other villages," said Onaroyaneh, the Bear clan mother. "They are short of food too. Unless we can get more food, our nation will starve this winter."

"Some of our crops may ripen late. At least that is something," said one woman. "How about the men? Can they do anything to help?"

"It will not be enough," said Ayonwaehs, the Mohawk war chief. He was angry and ashamed about the Algonquin raids.

"If the Algonquin have taken our food, let us take theirs!" cried one angry man. "Let Ayonwaehs lead a war band. Let us fight!" Several other people nodded and shouted their agreement. They were angry too.

"No."

As one, the villagers looked to their chief, Takarihoken, who was gazing into the fire.

"Why not?" exclaimed the angry man. "Are we warriors or cowards?"

Takarihoken looked up at the man. "We are warriors," he said calmly. "But we must not act rashly. The Algonquin were clearly after our food. This means that they have had a poor harvest too. They will protect their food at all costs. An attack now would risk much and gain us little."

The angry man nodded reluctantly. "What can we do, then?" he asked.

"The Mohawk Nation is in danger. Let us send a messenger to the Firekeepers and ask them to call the Grand Council together. Let us ask our brother nations for aid."

Around the fire, men and women were nodding in agreement. "Very well, then," said Onaroyaneh. "Ayonwaehs, please send messengers. We will leave soon."

As the villagers dispersed, Onaroyaneh went to sit near Takarihoken. "I am proud of you, Chief Takarihoken. You did well," she said.

"It may yet come to war," he replied. "Many people are angry."

"Yes," she agreed. "But war now would be madness. The clan mothers will not allow it."

37. Of all the Iroquois nations, the Mohawk were farthest to the
    A. east
    B. west
    C. north
    D. south

38. In the given story, a woman asks if the men can help. She is **not** asking if the men can
    A. go fishing
    B. hunt animals
    C. help harvest crops
    D. raid elsewhere for food

39. Takarihoken became chief of his Mohawk clan because
    A. he inherited the title from his father
    B. the people of his clan elected him
    C. the clan mother appointed him
    D. he was the clan's best warrior

40. Who were the Firekeepers?
    A. The Onondaga nation
    B. Iroquois spiritual leaders
    C. Experts in the Great Law
    D. The Grand Council chiefs

41. Onaroyaneh is **most likely** proud of Takarihoken because he displays
    A. respect
    B. wisdom
    C. courage
    D. compassion

42. Onaroyaneh is confident that the clan mothers will **not** allow a war. The clan mothers could prevent war by

    A. taking the chiefs' titles away

    B. overturning the chiefs' decision

    C. ordering the war chiefs to disobey

    D. withholding food from the warriors

Use the following information to answer the next three questions.

"The chiefs of the Onondaga welcome their brothers to the Grand Council," said Tadodaho. "Today, we meet to discuss a concern brought to us by Takarihoken of the Mohawk. We believe Takarihoken should act as spokesman. Does anyone object?" No one did.

Takarihoken explained the poor harvest and the Algonquin raids. "The Mohawk ask that you, our brother nations, come to our aid. Without food, we will starve. We would also ask that you send warriors to help us stop further raids, at least until winter comes."

The chiefs of the nations discussed the matter quietly amongst themselves. Soon, one of the Seneca chiefs rose to speak.

"The Seneca have had a great harvest of corn this season," said the chief. "We can share our harvest with the Mohawk, so they will not starve. However, we have no warriors to spare. Perhaps our Younger Brothers can help."

This sparked a lively discussion amongst the Oneida and Cayuga chiefs. The other chiefs waited patiently until they were finished.

"The lands of the Oneida are closest to the Mohawk," said a Cayuga chief. "Therefore, their warriors will arrive quickly. Let the Oneida send warriors to the Mohawk. The Cayuga are close to the Seneca. Our warriors will help carry the corn and guard it during transportation."

Tadodaho conferred with his fellow chiefs and nodded. "This is what is proposed. The Seneca will provide corn. The Cayuga will transport and guard it. The Oneida will send warriors to help guard Mohawk lands until the snows come. Chief Takarihoken, is this acceptable to the Mohawk?"

The Mohawk barely needed to confer at all. "It is, Tadodaho. We humbly thank our brothers."

43. This Grand Council meeting is an example of
   A. authoritarianism
   B. direct democracy
   C. representative democracy
   D. consensus decision making

44. The Seneca chief referred to the Oneida and Cayuga as "Younger Brothers" because the Oneida and Cayuga
   A. were the last to join the Confederacy
   B. had fewer chiefs than the other nations
   C. chiefs were younger than the Seneca chief
   D. nations were smaller than the other nations

45. The given passage shows that the Iroquois felt strongly about the importance of
   A. civility
   B. security
   C. generosity
   D. community

46. Athenian democracy is **most closely** associated with which of the following individuals?
   A. Cimon
   B. Pericles
   C. Socrates
   D. Miltiades

47. In ancient Athens, a metic was
   A. a law court official
   B. an open area in the city
   C. a foreigner living in Athens
   D. a general with the Athenian army

48. The Canadian Charter of Rights and Freedoms is based upon all of the following principles **except**

   A. equal opportunity

   B. representation

   C. fairness

   D. wealth

49. The **main** reason that collective rights are included in the Canadian Charter of Rights and Freedoms is to

   A. promote multiculturalism in Canada

   B. respect the historical and cultural contributions of Canadians

   C. strengthen the collective identity of particular groups of people in Canada

   D. ensure equality and fairness by maintaining the collective rights of particular groups

50. All of the following examples involve collective rights **except** for

   A. the rights of Francophones in Alberta

   B. the rights of Aboriginal peoples to lands or resources where treaties do not exist

   C. the right of Canadians to live in English-speaking or French-speaking communities

   D. the right to receive federal government services in the English language in a French community

ANSWERS AND SOLUTIONS—PRACTICE TEST

1. B	11. C	21. C	31. C	41. B
2. D	12. A	22. A	32. D	42. B
3. A	13. D	23. A	33. A	43. D
4. C	14. B	24. C	34. B	44. A
5. B	15. C	25. B	35. B	45. D
6. A	16. B	26. B	36. D	46. B
7. B	17. D	27. D	37. A	47. C
8. C	18. D	28. B	38. C	48. D
9. C	19. A	29. B	39. C	49. D
10. D	20. B	30. C	40. A	50. C

1. B

Direct democracy is when citizens vote on a particular issue directly. In Situation II, the students of Ms. Ebadi's class are voting directly for the charity they want to support the most.

2. D

Although the field trip sounds fun, the students in Ms. Westerlund's class have no choice about the location of the trip. Someone in authority has chosen the activities and when the activities will happen. There is no evidence that the students have had any input.

3. A

Chung is going to vote for someone. This person will represent the students on the student council. This is similar to the Canadian political system, where citizens vote for representatives at the local, provincial, and federal levels. It is called representative democracy.

4. C

Canadian citizens have the right to live and work anywhere in Canada. This is a mobility right, and it is protected by the Charter of Rights and Freedoms.

5. B

The Supreme Court of Canada ensures that laws in Canada follow the constitution and do not violate the Charter of Rights and Freedoms. The Supreme Court has final authority over interpretation of the Charter. They would certainly overturn any law restricting the mobility rights of Canadians.

6. A

Although many people might be offended by what the AFC is saying, AFC members have the right to free speech. As they are not making false claims to damage anyone's reputation, the members of the AFC are not abusing free speech. Although they must defer to the interpretation of the Supreme Court of Canada, provincial governments can and do interpret the Charter of Rights and Freedoms. If the provincial government did try to punish the AFC, the AFC could take their case to the Supreme Court.

7. B

The Treaty of La Grand Paix de Montréal was signed in 1701. Before this, the Haudenosaunee were almost constantly at war with the Algonquin and Ouendat. This war disrupted the fur trade. Also, the location of Montréal, on the traditional lands of the Algonquin, made it a potential target for Iroquois raids. To preserve the colony and the valuable fur trade, the French chose to broker, or act as a middleman for, a peace between the warring First Nations.

8. C

The Treaty of La Grand Paix de Montréal is remarkable because the French showed great respect for the First Nations and their collective identity. The French did not dictate terms, claim land, or otherwise impose themselves. Instead, they allowed the First Nations to negotiate on their own terms and reach an agreement that satisfied everyone. The First Nations were treated as equals, and the Treaty promised that their rights would be respected.

9. C

The Canadian Charter of Rights and Freedoms is entrenched. This means that it has been made part of the constitution. The Canadian Constitution represents the fundamental and most important laws of Canada. Charter rights and freedoms are among those essential laws that define Canada. The Charter applies at all levels of government. It can be changed, but it is extremely hard to do because that would mean changing the constitution. Although some Charter laws apply only to Canadian citizens, many of them also apply to foreigners in Canada, especially the legal and equality rights.

10. D

Candidate IV's priority is to prevent littering and vandalism. It is likely this will require the passage of new bylaws to prevent littering and allow the city government to fine offenders. Advertising of existing public services and hiring government employees such as police officers and healthcare professionals do not require new bylaws.

11. C

Health care is the responsibility of the provincial government, not the local government. The provincial Ministry of Health has a budget for all Alberta that they must balance. The ministry decides where the health care dollars are spent; mayors and county reeves can make spending requests, but the provincial government has the final say as to how the health care budget is spent. Therefore, Candidate III is the least likely to be able to deliver on his or her campaign promises.

12. A

Language immersion programs are usually run by public school boards. Although private schools may be run by committees, private school boards do not exist as government institutions. Separate school boards usually run schools with religious instruction, especially Catholic schools. Francophone school boards run schools where all the instruction is in French. These schools exist only where the Francophone population is high enough to warrant French-only schools.

13. D

All students in Alberta follow the same curriculum. It does not matter what school they go to or if they are home-schooled. The provincial Ministry of Education determines the curriculum.

14. B

Government committees are overseen by cabinet ministers. In the case of this bill, the minister would most likely be the Minister of the Environment. The executive council consists of the premier and the entire cabinet and does not directly oversee bill committees. MLAs may chair committees, but they must still answer to the minister. The lieutenant-governor is not involved with bill committees in any way.

15. C

The government has bills reviewed by committees to prepare them for the third reading. This allows the committee to answer any concerns or objections raised by MLAs or their constituents.

16. B

Although a bill does need the approval of the majority of the legislature, it only becomes a law when it is signed by the lieutenant-governor. The approval of the premier is not necessary. The Supreme Court is not involved in the law-making process.

17. D

Government services, such as health care or education, are the responsibility of the provincial government's ministries, not individual MLAs. Mr. Weinberg can, and likely will, advocate for his constituents, but he is not responsible for the delivery of services in his constituency.

18. D

Mr. Weinberg thinks about the tough questions opposition MLAs will have for him about the pollution bill. This means he is likely a part of the party in power. In Alberta, the Progressive Conservatives have held power since 1971.

19. A

The Figmenton Business Alliance is a lobby group. A lobby group works to influence government policy. Lobby groups organize so that they will be more effective in promoting the interests of their members. In the passage, Mr. Liao states that the FBA has been asking for the development. In other words, the FBA has been lobbying the government to promote the development.

20. B

The Figmenton Homeowners' Association is a grassroots organization. Grassroots movements generally start off small, with a few citizens who are concerned about a particular issue. In this case, citizens are concerned about their property values and increased traffic. Grassroots movements may not have the influence of a lobby group, but they have organized so that they will be more effective and united. Grassroots organizations can grow into powerful organizations. Many international non-governmental organizations started as grassroots organizations. However, with their local focus, the FHA is unlikely to become a non-governmental organization.

21. C

As a grassroots organization with a local focus, the Figmenton Homeowners' Association is unlikely to enjoy support outside the city.

As their names suggest, both the Organization of Alberta Motorists and the Alberta Environmental Protection Foundation cover the whole province.
The Figmenton Business Association is likely to enjoy the support of the outside businesses and customers they deal with. For example, suppliers, transportation companies, and so forth would likely support the FBA.

22. A

**The only provinces with French or bilingual government services are Quebec and New Brunswick. Federal government services are also available in French.
In Alberta, government affairs are conducted in English, although assistance is usually available for speakers of other languages. The Association canadienne-française de l'Alberta has focused on French cultural and educational programs, not on the delivery of government services.**

23. A

The Constitution Act, 1867, also known as the British North America Act, gave the new Canadian government complete authority over all Aboriginal peoples and lands within Canada's borders. The First Nations were not consulted. Earlier, the Treaty of La Grand Paix de Montréal and the Royal Proclamation had affirmed and upheld the rights of the First Nations. These rights would not be upheld again until the Constitution Act, 1982, and they are now part of the Charter of Rights and Freedoms.

24. C

First Nations authorities are responsible for such services as police, education, finance, and health.

25. B

Métis are persons who have both Aboriginal and European ancestry. For most of Canada's history, the Métis have struggled to gain recognition as a distinct group with their own unique culture and identity. Organizations, like the Métis Nation of Alberta Association, were formed to protect and promote the rights of the Métis.

26. B

The Métis were not officially recognized as a distinct Aboriginal group until the passage of the Constitution Act of 1982. None of the other given acts, proclamations, or treaties recognize the Métis as Aboriginal people.

27. D

Television or radio interviews can reach large audiences, but they can be expensive. Also, they are not targeted to a specific constituency. Newsletters, offices, and websites are all means by which MLAs can keep interested constituents up-to-date on government affairs, especially those affecting their constituency.

28. B

Magistrates were elected to judge cases in the law courts of Athens. They could also choose to pass cases on to be decided by juries. Magistrates had no religious function. They did not enforce the will of the Assembly. However, since the will of the Assembly was law, they might judge cases where someone had violated that will. The Assembly's agenda was prepared by councillors, who were members of the Council of 500.

29. B

The Spartan army was strong and well-trained. Every male Spartan was a soldier. The Spartans made the people they conquered grow food for them so they could focus on military training. The Spartan army was more than a match for the Athenian army. Sparta is roughly west of Athens. Although Sparta and Athens had earlier been allied against a massive invasion from Persia, they were bitter rivals and often fought.

30. C

Metics were people from other city-states who chose to live in Athens. They did not have as many rights, or as much legal protection, as citizens. However, metics could still prosper because Athens was a rich and powerful city.

31. C

Phostes and Ephialtes do not believe the Corinthian metic is really loyal to Athens. They still view him as a foreigner, and they do not trust his words.

32. D

In order to encourage citizens to participate in the Assembly, slaves would mark their clothing with red dye. Anyone with a red mark on their clothing had to go straight to the Assembly. If they did not, they would be fined.

33. A

The Assembly met atop the Pnyx, a hill with a flat top. There were benches and speaking platforms carved from the rock. Athens's theatres and temples were at the Acropolis. Many famous ancient buildings still stand there. The Athenians lived in the city itself, and the Pnyx was located a bit outside the city.

34. B

Except to attend or participate in religious ceremonies, Athenia women rarely left home. They did not attend Assembly meetings, gather crops, or work in shops.

35. B

Pericles was an Athenian general, or strategos. He is famous for his many improvements to Athenian politics and culture. He was also a skilled public speaker and a popular statesman.

36. D

In ancient Athens, the decision of the Assembly was final. Pericles, though very powerful, did not rule Athens. He could speak at the Assembly and try to sway the citizens, but he could not do more than that. The Council was important in the day-to-day running of Athens and could propose a course of action, but it could not make the final decision. The generals would have to do their best to carry out the will of the Assembly if it chose to go to war.

37. A

The Mohawk nation was the easternmost nation of the Confederacy. To the west of the Mohawk were the Oneida. After the Oneida were the Onondaga, Cayuga, and Seneca.

38. C

In Iroquois culture, men were not involved in farming. The land belonged to the women, and it was the women who planted, tended, and harvested the crops. Men could fish, hunt, or raid other First Nations for food, but they would not help with the harvest.

39. C

The right to appoint or remove chiefs belonged to the clan mothers. Therefore, Takarihoken was chosen by the clan mother, Onaroyaneh.

40. A

The Onondaga were the hosts of the Grand Council. When an issue arose, the Onondaga chiefs decided whether it was important enough to be considered by the Grand Council or not. As part of their ceremonial duties, they tended the fire in the Grand Council lodge. Thus, they were the Firekeepers.

41. B

Takarihoken remains calm and uses his head when he answers the angry man. He displays wisdom. Wisdom was one of the most important qualities for a chief to possess.

42. B

The Great Law of Peace allowed the clan mothers to overturn any decision relating to a war or a treaty made by the Grand Council. Therefore, if the Grand Council declared war, the clan mothers could legally overturn the decision without resorting to other acts, such as removing the chiefs from power or withholding food from the warriors.

43. D

The Grand Council uses consensus, or reaching an agreement, to make decisions. Since everyone must agree to the decision, it is not an authoritarian system. However, it is not a democratic system because no voting is involved.

44. A

The Oneida and Cayuga joined the Confederacy after the Onondaga, Mohawk, and Seneca. They were called the Younger Brothers. The Younger Brothers actually had more chiefs than the Mohawk and Seneca. The number of chiefs, the age of the chiefs, and the size of the nation were all unimportant in the Grand Council.

45. D

In Iroquois culture, the community was always important. Rather than working for their own personal benefit, the Iroquois worked to meet the needs of the community. The community could include the village, the clan, the nation, or the whole Confederacy. In the passage, the other nations offer to help the Mohawk to the best of their abilities. The Seneca chief, for example, does not expect repayment for the corn. He is not being generous. He is simply acting for the benefit of the Confederacy.

46. B

Although Pericles was not the founder of Athenian democracy, he helped shape it. Today, many scholars call Athens's democratic period the Age of Pericles or Periclean Athens.

Cimon was a political rival of Pericles. Socrates was a philosopher who was put on trial for his views—they were seen as dangerous. Today, Socrates is among the most famous philosophers of all time. Miltiades was a general who defeated a Persian invasion of Greece.

47. C

Metics were foreigners who lived in Athens. They were free to live and work as they chose. However, they could not own land or participate in government, no matter how long they lived in Athens.

Law court officials were called magistrates. Open areas in the city were called agorae. Athenian generals were called strategoi.

48. D

Wealth is not a principle. Principles are strongly held values of what is important in our Canadian democratic society.

Equal opportunity for all, representation (by elected individuals), and fairness (justice) are principles upon which the Charter is based.

49. D

The main reason that collective rights are included in the Charter is to ensure equality and fairness by maintaining the historic and constitutional rights of particular groups in Canada. Thus, the Charter protects collective rights for Aboriginal groups and the linguistic rights of official language minorities throughout Canada.

Canada is a country of many cultures. However, collective rights are not included in the Canadian Charter of Rights and Freedoms in order to promote multiculturalism in Canada. Many Canadians, of many cultures, have made contributions during Canada's history. A collective identity is held by groups that share common beliefs, and often the same language, culture, and values. Although a group's collective identity may be strengthened by the recognition of their collective rights in the Charter, the main reason that collective rights are included is to ensure equality and fairness.

50. C

The right of Canadian citizens to live in English-speaking or French-speaking communities is a mobility right (the right to move to other provinces or choose other forms of work), not a collective right.

Collective rights include the linguistic rights of official language minorities (English-speaking and French-speaking people) in Canada. A Francophone (French-speaking person) living in Alberta (majority English-speaking province) would have certain collective rights, such as the right to French education where enough French people live in a community to warrant it. Historic references to the collective rights of Canada's Aboriginal peoples are included in the Charter and the Constitution Act (1982). These rights are considered when Aboriginal groups seek title to lands in Canada or compensation for lands given up (land claims). Specific land claims concern original treaties that have been broken or not fulfilled. Comprehensive land claims concern Aboriginal claims to lands and natural resources in areas where treaties have never existed. Federal government services are provided in either of Canada's official languages, French or English. Customers have the right to choose in which official language they wish to receive services.

NOTES

Written Response

WRITTEN RESPONSE

Use the following information to answer the next question.

A passage from a political speech is given.

"We, as Canadians, are luckier than most of us know. We live in a nation of laws, freedoms, tolerance, equity, and justice. We live in a stable society, where most of our fellow citizens can live in peace and prosperity. We have universal healthcare and education, a strong economy, and a democratic government. We are known around the world for being fair, open minded, and accepting of different cultures.

"Imagine living in another country, where there are none of these things. Imagine a country where poverty and sickness are widespread, the people are oppressed by their government, and war and chaos are always possible. Imagine a country where women and minorities are discriminated against and basic human rights are not respected.

"Canada is special. We enjoy a level of freedom and prosperity most of the world can only dream of. Sadly, many Canadians do not realize that all our rights and freedoms come with certain responsibilities. I'm not just talking about the obvious things, like obeying laws or paying taxes. I'm talking about actively participating in Canada and making a difference in our communities, in our politics, and in our culture.

"John F. Kennedy said it best. 'Ask not what your country can do for you—ask what you can do for your country.' Think about what you, as a Canadian, can do for Canada. It's easy to do the bare minimum. Let us think about what more we can do, as responsible Canadian citizens."

1. In light of the given speech, what are the responsibilities of Canadian citizens?

_____

_____

_____

_____

_____

_____

_____

_____

_____

Use the following information to answer the next question.

Markus and his friends liked to hang out at James Kaye Park. It had an open field for soccer or football, a couple of basketball hoops, and a sandlot. But lately, the park had been getting pretty rundown. There were thistles and big patches of bare ground in the field. The backboard on one of the basketball hoops was cracked, and this made the ball bounce funny. The sandlot was full of litter, which had been there for ages.

"Man," said Markus, "this place needs work!"

"Sure does," said Piotr, kicking at the turf. "Look at the size of this divot! Someone could get hurt!"

"Yeah, it is getting to be a real dump too," said Carrie-Anne. "Maybe we should find someplace else to hang out."

"There has got to be something we can do!" protested Yash. "I like this place!"

Piotr snorted. "What, are you going to pick thistles and buy a new backboard?"

"Very funny. I mean that we can ask the government for help," replied Yash.

"The government? Yash, we are kids. We cannot vote. They are not going to listen to us."

"Yes, they will! Our parents vote, remember? Besides, it is the government's job to listen to people."

"I agree with Yash," said Carrie-Anne. "This is a public park. It should be clean and safe."

"Okay, C.A.," said Markus. "But how do we get the government to listen? What should we do?"

2. The kids will try to get the government to take care of James Kaye Park. How should they proceed?

_____

_____

_____

_____

_____

_____

_____

Use the following information to answer the next question.

Ms. Ebadi's class were learning about ancient Athens and the Iroquois. Ms. Ebadi asked two of her students which political system they thought was better.

Student 1

I think the ancient Athenians had a better system. First of all, it was a democracy, and all citizens were equals. They could vote directly on issues. The government had to obey the will of the people. The judges and councillors were chosen by lottery, so every citizen had the chance to serve the city. If you look at the Iroquois system, they could not vote at all. It was not a democracy. The clan mothers and chiefs basically made all the decisions for their people.

Student 2

I think the Iroquois had a better system. I like the idea of consensus decision making. It means that everyone's opinion, not just the opinion of the majority, mattered. The chiefs were there to represent their communities. The clan mothers made sure they did a good job. Women and men both had political power. In ancient Athens, only male citizens could vote. Women, metics, and slaves had no say in politics.

---

3. With which student do you agree? Why?

_____

_____

_____

_____

_____

_____

_____

_____

_____

Appendices

GLOSSARY OF TERMS

Agora	A wide, open area in the middle of the city that served as a marketplace.
Assembly	The main decision-making body of Athenian democracy. Every male citizen could participate in the Assembly. Decisions were made according to the will of the majority.
Attica	The area of Greece dominated by the city-state of Athens. Normally, only people from one of the ten tribes of Attica could become citizens.
Boule	The Greek name for the Council of 500.
Bouleterion	The meeting place of the Council of 500.
Chief	One of the political leaders of the Iroquois. Chiefs were chosen by the clan mothers, who had hereditary ownership of the title. In each Iroquois nation, there was one chief from each clan within the nation.
City-State	A city that has all the powers of an independent nation. In ancient Greece, powerful city-states often dominated the area around them as well.
Clan	A group of Iroquois who considered one another family, even if they were not blood relatives. Clans were named after animals, such as Wolf or Turtle. Each clan was led by a clan mother. Members of different Iroquois nations could belong to the same clan.
Clan mother	The hereditary leader of an Iroquois clan. Clan mothers "owned" the title of chief, which she could give or take away as she chose.
Collective Rights; Collective Identity	Belong to individuals who together form a particular group. Groups that share common beliefs and often the same language, culture, and values.
Confederacy	A political body made up of multiple nations or states.
Council of 500	A democratic decision-making body. The Council, or boule, advised the Assembly, helped prepare its agenda, and dealt with emergencies.
Democracy	A form of government in which the power resides in the people.
Democratic Freedoms	Ensure Canadians the right to vote for representatives in federal and provincial governments.
Demos	Formally, the citizens of a city-state such as Athens. Informally, the ancient Greek word for "people."
Direct Democracy	Government is based on the citizens themselves voting directly on political matters.
Elder Brothers	The Mohawk and Seneca Nations, who were the first to join the Confederacy.
Equality Rights	Ensure equal and fair treatment to everyone. Equality rights involve treating all individuals equally regardless of religious choice, race, ethnic or national origin, cognitive or physical impairments, age, or gender.
Faithkeeper	A person responsible for the spiritual life of the Iroquois people. Faithkeepers led Iroquois ceremonies and remembered Iroquois legends.
Firekeepers	The Onondaga Nation, who hosted the Grand Council of the Iroquois Confederacy.
Fundamental Freedoms	Include the freedom of speech, thought, opinion, and religion.
Grand Council	The main political body of the Iroquois, comprising 50 chiefs from the five original nations. The Grand Council made decisions by consensus.
Great Law of Peace	The governing law of the Iroquois; essentially, their constitution.
Haudenosaunee	The Iroquois name for themselves. Literally, "people of the longhouse."

Hiawatha	An important figure in Iroquois legends; he helped the Peacemaker to convince the original Five Nations to accept the Great Law of Peace.
Legal Rights	Ensure the safety of Canadians and protect citizens involved in legal conflict.
Longhouse	The traditional dwelling (living space) of the Iroquois.
Magistrate	A person who heard cases in the law courts of Athens. The magistrate could judge the case himself, or refer it to a jury.
Metic	A foreign-born person living in Athens. Metics were free, but could not participate in Athens's democracy.
Mobility Rights	Allow all citizens with permanent residency status in Canada the right to live, work, and travel anywhere in the country.
Olympia	A sacred site in southwest Greece. The original Olympic Games were held here to honour the god Zeus. Not to be confused with Mt. Olympus, a mountain in northern Greece.
Ostracism	The practice of exiling (forcing to leave) a person based on a majority vote in the Assembly. Today, ostracism means to exclude or banish someone from a group.
Peacemaker	A Huron man named Deganawidah who brought the Great Law of Peace to the Iroquois.
Pericles	An Athenian general and leader. Pericles is the person most associated with Athenian democracy and Athens's "golden age" of philosophy and art.
Pine tree chief	A man with great ability appointed by the Grand Council. Pine tree chiefs were to use their gifts for the good of the Iroquois.
Pnyx	The meeting place of the Assembly; a large, open area on the outskirts of ancient Athens.
Representative Democracy	Allows citizens to use their right to vote to elect a representative who will express their concerns and make political decisions for them.
Sparta	A city in southwest Greece. In ancient times, the city-state of Sparta was Athens's main rival for power in Greece, and fought often. All Spartan males were soldiers; the work of farming, building, and so forth was done by captured prisoners of war.
Tadodaho	In Iroquois legend, an evil chief who initially refused to accept the Great Peace until Hiawatha convinced him. Today, Tadodaho is the title given to the spiritual leader of the Six Nations.
Three Sisters	Bean, corns, and squash: the main food source of the Iroquois.
Wampum	Coloured shells. The Iroquois strung wampum together, or made wampum belts. Wampum strings and belts have great ceremonial, spiritual, and historical importance to the Iroquois.
War chief	A man appointed by the Council as war leaders. War chiefs could also convey warnings to the Council if the clan mothers felt that they were breaking the Great Law of Peace.
Younger Brothers	The Oneida and Cayuga Nations, who joined the Confederacy after the Mohawk and Seneca.

CREDITS

Every effort has been made to provide proper acknowledgement of the original source and to comply with copyright law. However, some attempts to establish original copyright ownership may have been unsuccessful. If copyright ownership can be identified, please notify Castle Rock Research Corp so that appropriate corrective action can be taken.

Some images in this document are from www.clipart.com, © 2013 Clipart.com, a division of Getty Images.

NOTES

BOOK ORDERING INFORMATION

ELEMENTARY and JUNIOR HIGH TITLES

Castle Rock Research offers the following resources to support Alberta students. You can order any of these materials online at:

www.castlerockresearch.com/store

SOLARO - Online Learning		The KEY	SNAP	Prob Solved	Class Notes
$29.95 ea.*		$29.95 ea.*	$29.95 ea.*	$19.95 ea.*	$19.95 ea.*
English Language Arts 9	English Language Arts 6	English Language Arts 9	Science 9	Science 9	Science 9
English Language Arts 8	English Language Arts 5	English Language Arts 6	Mathematics 9	Mathematics 9	Mathematics 9
English Language Arts 7	English Language Arts 4	English Language Arts 3	Mathematics 8	Mathematics 8	Mathematics 8
Mathematics 9	English Language Arts 3	Mathematics 9	Mathematics 7	Mathematics 7	Mathematics 7
Mathematics 8	Mathematics 6	Mathematics 8	Mathematics 6		
Mathematics 7	Mathematics 5	Mathematics 7	Mathematics 5		
Science 9	Mathematics 4	Mathematics 6	Mathematics 4		
Science 8	Mathematics 3	Mathematics 4	Mathematics 3		
Science 7	Science 6	Mathematics 3			
Social Studies 9	Science 5	Science 9			
Social Studies 6	Science 4	Science 6			
	Science 3	Social Studies 9			
		Social Studies 6			

*Prices do not include taxes or shipping.

Study online using **SOLARO,** with access to multiple courses available by either a monthly or an annual subscription.

The KEY Study Guide is specifically designed to assist students in preparing for unit tests, final exams, and provincial examinations.

The **Student Notes and Problems (SNAP) Workbook** contains complete explanations of curriculum concepts, examples, and exercise questions.

The **Problem Solved** contains exercise questions and complete solutions.

The **Class Notes** contains complete explanations of curriculum concepts.

If you would like to order Castle Rock resources for your school, please visit our school ordering page:

www.castlerockresearch.com/school-orders/